I0426026

March 2012

STATE AND LOCAL GOVERNMENT PENSION PLANS

Economic Downturn Spurs Efforts to Address Costs and Sustainability

GAO

Accountability * Integrity * Reliability

GAO-12-322

Highlights of GAO-12-322, a report to congressional requesters

STATE AND LOCAL GOVERNMENT PENSION PLANS

Economic Downturn Spurs Efforts to Address Costs and Sustainability

Why GAO Did This Study

Over 27 million employees and beneficiaries are covered by state and local government pension plans. However, the recent economic downturn and associated budget challenges confronting state and local governments pose some questions as to the sustainability of these plans, and what changes, if any, state and local governments are making to strengthen the financial condition of their pension plans. GAO was asked to examine

(1) recent trends in the financial condition of state and local government pension plans and

(2) strategies state and local governments are using to manage pension costs and the impacts of these strategies on plans, sponsors, employees, and retirees.

To address these topics, GAO analyzed various measures of sector-wide financial condition based on national-level data on pension funding from the U.S. Census Bureau and others, and reviewed information on recent state legislative changes affecting government pensions from annual reports prepared by the National Conference of State Legislatures (NCSL). GAO did not assess the soundness of individual plans, but did obtain documents and conduct interviews with pension and budget officials in eight states and eight localities, selected to illustrate the range of strategies being implemented to meet current and future pension funding requirement.

The Internal Revenue Service and Social Security Administration provided technical comments, which were incorporated, as appropriate.

View GAO-12-322. For more information, contact Barbara D. Bovbjerg at (202) 512-7215 or bovbjergb@gao.gov, or Stanley J. Czerwinski at (202) 512-6806 or czerwinskis@gao.gov.

What GAO Found

Despite the recent economic downturn, most large state and local government pension plans have assets sufficient to cover benefit payments to retirees for a decade or more. However, pension plans still face challenges over the long term due to the gap between assets and liabilities. In the past, some plan sponsors have not made adequate plan contributions or have granted unfunded benefit increases, and many suffered from investment losses during the economic downturn. The resulting gap between asset values and projected liabilities has led to steady increases in the actuarially required contribution levels needed to help sustain pension plans at the same time state and local governments face other fiscal pressures.

Since 2008, the combination of fiscal pressures and increasing contribution requirements has spurred many states and localities to take action to strengthen the financial condition of their plans for the long term, often packaging multiple changes together. GAO's tabulation of recent state legislative changes reported by NCSL and review of reforms in selected sites revealed the following:

- **Reducing benefits:** 35 states have reduced pension benefits, mostly for future employees due to legal provisions protecting benefits for current employees and retirees. A few states, like Colorado, have reduced postretirement benefit increases for all members and beneficiaries of their pension plans.
- **Increasing member contributions:** Half of the states have increased member contributions, thereby shifting a larger share of pension costs to employees.
- **Switching to a hybrid approach:** Georgia, Michigan, and Utah recently implemented hybrid approaches, which incorporate a defined contribution plan component, shifting some investment risk to employees.

At the same time, some states and localities have also adjusted their funding practices to help manage pension contribution requirements in the short term by changing actuarial methods, deferring contributions, or issuing bonds, actions that may increase future pension costs. Going forward, growing budget pressures will continue to challenge state and local governments' abilities to provide adequate contributions to help sustain their pension plans.

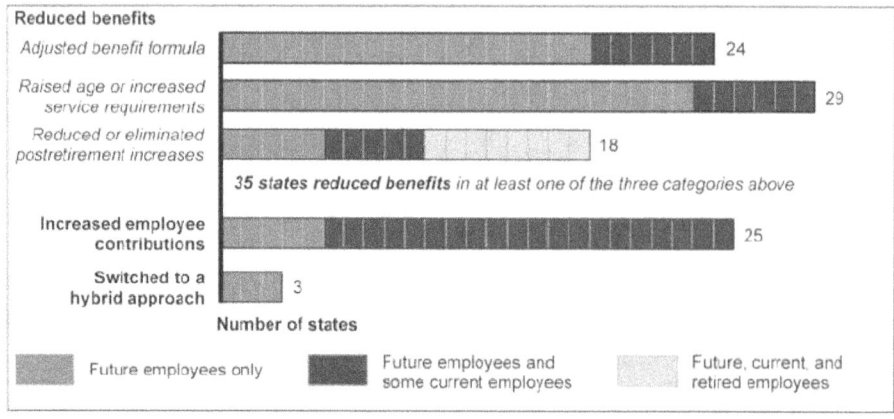

Notable Changes to State-Sponsored Pension Plans (January 2008 to June 2011)

Source: GAO analysis of annual NCSL reports.

_____ **United States Government Accountability Office**

Contents

Abbreviations

ARC	annual required contribution
ASB	Actuarial Standards Board
CAFR	Comprehensive Annual Financial Report
COLA	cost-of-living adjustment
CPI-W	Consumer Price Index for Urban Wage Earners and Clerical Workers
ERISA	Employee Retirement Income Security Act of 1974
GAAP	generally accepted accounting principles
GASB	Governmental Accounting Standards Board
NASBO	National Association of State Budget Officers
NCSL	National Conference of State Legislatures
POB	pension obligation bond

United States Government Accountability Office
Washington, DC 20548

March 2, 2012

The Honorable Herb Kohl
Chairman
Special Committee on Aging
United States Senate

The Honorable Michael B. Enzi
Ranking Member
Committee on Health, Education,
Labor, and Pensions
United States Senate

The recent economic downturn combined with continuing budget challenges has heightened concerns about the financial condition of state and local pension plans. Pension funding is a long-term endeavor, but states and local governments often have annual balanced budget requirements that can pit government contributions to pension plans against other pressing funding needs. Although state and local retiree benefits are not subject, for the most part, to federal laws governing private sector retiree benefits, the federal government has an interest in ensuring that all Americans have a secure retirement. This includes the over 27 million people covered by state and local government pension plans.[1] The federal government also has an interest in the challenging fiscal situation facing the state and local sectors because fiscal health presents a national challenge shared by all levels of government. In light of these concerns, you asked us to examine

1. recent trends in the financial condition of state and local government pension plans and

2. strategies state and local governments are using to manage pension costs and the impacts of these strategies on plans, sponsors, employees, and retirees.

---

[1]This total is based on the U.S. Census Bureau's 2009 Survey of State and Local Public-Employee Retirement Systems and includes active members, inactive members, and beneficiaries.

To describe trends in the financial condition of state and local pension funds, we analyzed various measures of sector-wide financial condition based on existing national-level data on pension funding. We analyzed data from the U.S. Census Bureau's surveys of state and local retirement systems and from the Public Plans Database developed by the Boston College Center for Retirement Research, which includes financial data on 126 large state and local defined benefit plans covering more than 85 percent of total state and local government pension assets and members. To better understand the context for these trends, we reviewed existing literature on state and local government pension plans and interviewed national experts on state and local government pension issues.

To identify the prevalence of various strategies state and local governments are using to manage pension costs, we analyzed national-level data on state legislative changes and use of bonds to finance their plans. Specifically, to identify legislative changes, we analyzed annual reports prepared by the National Conference of State Legislatures (NCSL) summarizing selected state pension and retirement legislation enacted from January 1, 2008, through June 30, 2011.[2] We limited our analysis of these NCSL reports to changes affecting broad categories of employees, such as state employees, teachers, public safety personnel, and local employees who are members of state-administered plans. In some limited instances, to better understand a legislative change, we reviewed supplemental documents such as pension plan documents and summaries of the legislation prepared by plans, state legislative counsel, or state agencies. We did not conduct an independent legal analysis to verify the accuracy of the information pertaining to recently enacted legislation contained in the NCSL reports. To identify bonds issued for the purpose of financing public pension plans, we analyzed multiple sources of bond data, including Mergent BondViewer and the Electronic Municipal Market Access system.[3] We supplemented these national-level data by interviewing state and local pension and budget officials, and reviewing financial and actuarial reports, from a small judgmental sample of plans from eight states, and one locality within each of these states, that had

---

[2]Ronald K. Snell, NCSL, *Pensions and Retirement Plan Enactments,* annual reports for 2008-2010 and 2011 report as of June 30, 2011. For additional information about the state legislative changes described in this report, refer to the NCSL reports.

[3]Mergent BondViewer is an online database of bond data. The Electronic Municipal Market Access system, maintained by the Municipal Securities Rulemaking Board, is an online database of municipal disclosures and data on the municipal securities market

GAO-12-322 State and Local Pensions

implemented pension modifications since 2008 (see table 1). This judgmental sample was selected to provide examples of plans experiencing a range of financial conditions and types of strategies adopted by their sponsors. We based this selection on our analysis of NCSL annual reports on pension legislation and suggestions from our interviews with pension experts. We did not assess the financial soundness of individual plans.

Table 1: State and Local Plans Selected for Review

State	State plan	Locality	Local plan
California	• California State Teachers' Retirement System • California Public Employees' Retirement System	Sonoma County	Sonoma County Employees' Retirement Association
Colorado	• Colorado Public Employees' Retirement Association	City of Denver	Denver Employees Retirement Plan
Georgia	• Employees' Retirement System of Georgia	Cobb County	Cobb County Employees' Retirement System Pension Plan
Illinois	• State Employees' Retirement System of Illinois • Teachers' Retirement System of the State of Illinois	City of Chicago	Policemen's Annuity and Benefit Fund of Chicago
Missouri	• Missouri State Employees' Retirement System • Missouri Department of Transportation and Highway Patrol Employees' Retirement System	City of Springfield	Police Officers' and Firefighters' Retirement Fund
Pennsylvania	• Pennsylvania Public School Employees' Retirement System • Pennsylvania State Employees' Retirement System	City of Philadelphia	City of Philadelphia Municipal Pension Plan
Utah	• Utah Retirement Systems	City of Bountiful	Public Safety Retirement System (City of Bountiful)- part of the Utah Retirement Systems
Virginia	• Virginia Retirement System	City of Norfolk	Employees' Retirement System of the City of Norfolk

Source: GAO.

Note: See appendix I for more detailed profiles of each state, locality, and plan.

We conducted this performance audit from December 2010 to March 2012 in accordance with generally accepted government auditing standards. Those standards require that we plan and perform the audit to obtain sufficient, appropriate evidence to provide a reasonable basis for our findings and conclusions based on our audit objectives. We believe that the evidence obtained provides a reasonable basis for our findings and conclusions based on our audit objectives.

Background

There are over 3,400 state and local pension systems in the United States, according to the most recent Census Bureau Survey of State and Local Public-Employee Retirement Systems.[4] Most large plans are state plans, and more state and local employees are covered by state-administered plans than by locally-administered plans (about 24 million members and beneficiaries compared with about 3 million). However, there are more local government employees than state government employees (about 14 million compared with about 5 million), and while local governments sometimes participate in plans administered by states, the local governments generally retain responsibility for contributing the employer's share of funding to the plans for their employees. As a result, local governments contribute more to pension plans each state fiscal year, overall, than do state governments (see fig. 1).[5]

Figure 1: State and Local Government Pension Contributions, Fiscal Year 2009

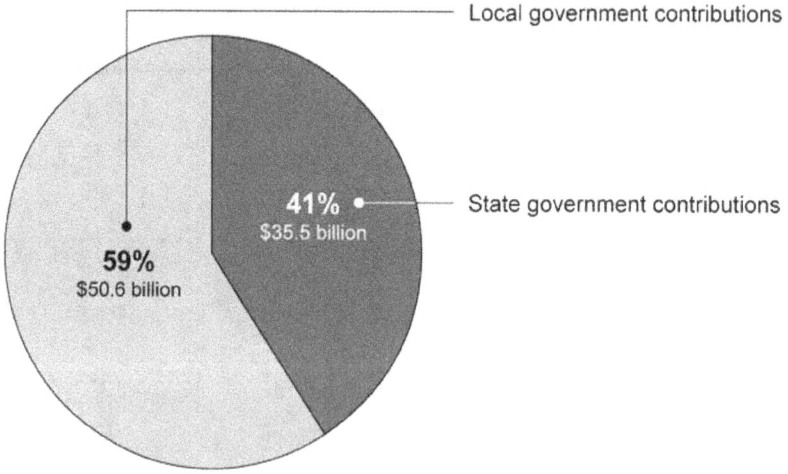

Source: GAO analysis of U.S. Census data.

Pension plans are generally characterized as either defined benefit or defined contribution plans. Unlike in the private sector, defined benefit

---

[4]U.S. Census, *2009 Survey of State and Local Public-Employee Retirement Systems* (Washington, D.C. 2011).

[5]Throughout this report, the term "fiscal year" refers to state fiscal year (as opposed to federal fiscal year). State fiscal years vary, but most run from July 1 to June 30, according to the Census Bureau.

plans provide primary pension benefits for most state and local government workers. About 78 percent of state and local employees participated in defined benefit plans in 2011, compared with only 18 percent of private sector employees.[6] In a defined benefit plan, the amount of the benefit payment is determined by a formula (in the public sector, the formula is typically based on the retiree's years of service and final average salary, and is most often provided as a lifetime annuity). However, unlike private sector employees with defined benefit plans, state and local government employees generally contribute to their defined benefit plans. A few states offer defined contribution or other types of retirement plans as the primary retirement plan.[7] In a defined contribution plan, the key determinants of the benefit amount are the member's and employer's contribution rates, and the rate of return achieved on the investments in an individual's account over time. Alternatively, some states have adopted hybrid approaches that combine components of both defined benefit and defined contribution plans.

Also unlike in the private sector, many state and local employees are not covered by Social Security. About 6.4 million, or over one-fourth, of state and local government employees are not eligible to receive Social Security benefits based on their government earnings and do not pay Social Security taxes on earnings from their government occupations.[8] As a result, employer-provided pension benefits for non-covered employees are generally higher than for employees covered by Social Security, and employee and employer contributions are higher as well.

---

[6]U.S. Department of Labor, Bureau of Labor Statistics, *National Compensation Survey: Employee Benefits in the United States*, March 2011 (Washington, D.C.: 2011).

[7]As we have previously reported, all states also offer a voluntary, supplemental defined contribution option in addition to their primary defined benefit plan. See GAO, *State and Local Government Retiree Benefits: Current Status of Benefit Structures, Protections, and Fiscal Outlook for Funding Future Costs*, GAO-07-1156 (Washington, D.C.: Sept. 24, 2007).

[8]42 U.S.C. § 410(a)(7). Historically, Social Security did not require coverage of government employment. In 1950, Congress enacted legislation allowing voluntary coverage to state and local government employees not covered by public pension plans, and in 1955, extended voluntary coverage to those already covered by plans as well. Social Security Act Amendments of 1950, Pub. L. No. 809, § 106, 64 Stat. 477 (1950), codified at 42 U.S.C. § 218(a) &(d); Social Security Amendments of 1956, Pub. L. No. 880, § 211 (e), 70 Stat. 807 (1956), codified at 42 U.S.C. § 218(d)(6).

The federal government has not imposed the same funding and reporting requirements on state and local pensions as it has on private sector pension plans.[9] State and local government pension plans are not covered by most of the substantive requirements under the Employee Retirement Income Security Act of 1974 (ERISA)—requirements which apply to most private employer benefit plans. Nor are they insured by the Pension Benefit Guaranty Corporation as private plans are. Federal law generally does not require state and local governments to prefund or report on the funded status of pension plans. However, in order for participants to receive preferential tax treatment (that is, for employee contributions and investment earnings to be tax-deferred), state and local pensions must comply with certain requirements of the Internal Revenue Code.[10]

State and local governments also follow different standards than the private sector for accounting and financial reporting. The Governmental Accounting Standards Board (GASB), an independent organization, has been recognized by governments, the accounting industry, and the capital markets as the official source of generally accepted accounting principles (GAAP) for U.S. state and local governments. GASB's standards are not federal laws or regulations and GASB does not have enforcement authority. However, compliance with its standards is enforced through laws of some individual states and the audit process, whereby auditors render opinions on the fair presentation of state and local governments'

---

[9]To further clarify the difference between government and private sector pension plans, the Internal Revenue Service issued an advance notice of proposed rulemaking in November 2011 relating to the definition of the term "governmental plan." The guidance under consideration is intended to establish coordinated criteria for determining whether a plan is a governmental plan and address current uncertainty regarding entities with organizational, regulatory, and contractual connections with states or political subdivisions of states. Determination of Governmental Plan Status, 76 Fed. Reg. 69,172 (Nov. 8, 2011), to be codified at 26 C.F.R. § 1.414(d)-1.

[10]Contributions to qualified pension plans that meet certain requirements—whether defined benefit or defined contribution—are generally not counted as taxable income to employees when the contributions are made. However, when pension benefits are paid, amounts not previously taxed are subject to federal and perhaps state tax. This also applies to the interest income such contributions generate. As an alternative, some state and local qualified pension plans provide an option for designated Roth contributions to Roth accounts, and such contributions to Roth accounts are made after taxation. The interest income earned on such contributions is generally not subject to tax upon distribution, provided that the requirements and restrictions applicable to such accounts under the Internal Revenue Code have been satisfied.

financial statements in conformity with GAAP. GASB's standards require reporting financial information on pensions, such as the annual pension cost, contributions actually made to the plan, and the ratio of assets to liabilities. In addition, actuarial standards of practice are promulgated by the Actuarial Standards Board. These standards are designed to provide practicing actuaries with a basis for assuring that their work will conform to appropriate practices and to assure the public that actuaries are professionally accountable (see app. II for information on recently proposed changes to GASB and Actuarial Standards Board standards).

Some municipal bond analysts have reported concerns about state and local governments' creditworthiness in light of the recent economic downturn and continuing pension obligations. In 2008 and 2010, respectively, the Securities and Exchange Commission took enforcement actions against the city of San Diego and the state of New Jersey for misrepresenting the financial condition of their pension funds in information provided to investors.[11]

Plans Have Sufficient Assets to Pay Near-Term Benefits, but Growing Budget Pressures Will Challenge Their Sustainability

Although pension plans suffered significant investment losses from the recent economic downturn, which was the most serious since the Great Depression, most state and local government plans currently have assets sufficient to cover their benefit commitments for a decade or more. Nevertheless, most plans have experienced a growing gap between actuarial assets and liabilities over the past decade, meaning that higher contributions from government sponsors are needed to maintain funds on an actuarially based path toward sustainability. In spite of budget pressures through the recession, most plans continued to receive prerecession contribution levels on an actuarial basis from their sponsors, with most plans contributing their full actuarial level. However, there were some notable exceptions, and these plans continued to receive lower contribution payments. State and local governments experienced declining revenues and growing expenses on other fronts, and growing budget pressures will continue to challenge their ability to provide adequate contributions to help sustain their pension funds.

---

[11]GAO is conducting work under Section 976 of the Dodd-Frank Wall Street Reform and Consumer Protection Act, enacted in 2010, to study the information that state and local governments provide investors in municipal securities, including the advantages and disadvantages of providing additional financial information. The report is scheduled for issuance in summer 2012.

Despite Investment Losses, Most Plans Hold Sufficient Assets to Pay Benefit Obligations for the Near Future

The recent economic downturn resulted in state and local pension plans suffering significant investment losses. Positive investment returns are an important source of funds for pension plans, and have historically generated more than half of state and local pension fund increases. However, rather than adding to plans' assets, investments lost more than $672 billion during fiscal years 2008 and 2009, based upon Census Bureau figures for the sector (see fig. 2). Since 2009, improvements in investment earnings have helped plans recover some of these losses, as evidenced by more recent Census Bureau data on large plans.[12] More importantly, however, public pension plans have built up assets over many years through prefunding (that is, employer and member contributions) and through the accumulation of associated investment returns.[13]

---

[12]Based on Census quarterly data on 100 large retirement systems, investment returns have been mostly positive since the second quarter of 2009. See Census, *Finances of Selected State and Local Government Employee Retirement Systems*.

[13]A prefunded plan means a plan has set aside funds for pension obligations made for current employees as opposed to pay-as-you go plan, which does not set aside funds to pay for future obligations to current employees.

Figure 2: Investment Returns for State and Local Government Pension Plans, Fiscal Years 2005–2009

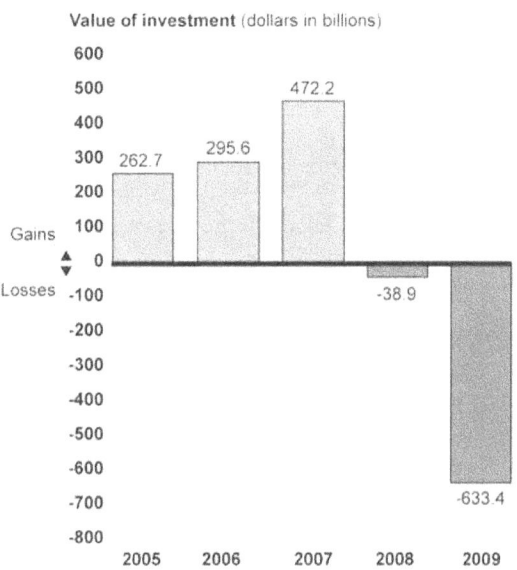

Source: State and local retirement systems data from Census Bureau

Assessing the financial condition across all plans using actuarially determined figures (such as a plan's funded ratio) is challenging, in part, because of the various methods and assumptions used by these plans (see app. II). One alternative measure of financial condition across pension plans, although not optimal when assessing the financial health of a single plan, is the ratio of fund assets to annual expenditures.[14] Fund assets represent the dollar amount a plan has built up, while annual expenditures ultimately determine how quickly assets are spent down.[15] Alternatively, when assessing the financial condition of an individual defined benefit plan, various approaches are used, and looking at multiple factors is especially useful in providing a more complete picture of a plan's financial condition. In addition to the level of funding (level of plan assets relative to plan liabilities), assessments of a plan's financial

---

[14]Expenditures include both annual benefit payments and any expenses paid out of plan assets.

[15]However, using nonactuarial figures is a simplification because it does not consider the unique demographic profile—especially, the relative proportions of retired and active workers in the plan's actuarial liability—and related data associated with each plan.

GAO-12-322 State and Local Pensions

viability by rating agencies and others may take into consideration the influence of the plan sponsor, the plan's underlying methods and assumptions, and efforts to manage risk (see table 2).

Table 2: Understanding the Financial Condition of a Public Defined Benefit Plan

	Sample questions
Influence of plan sponsor	• Has the government sponsor maintained its actuarial required contributions over time?
	• What is the outlook for the government sponsor's economy and budget (to afford future contributions)?
	• Is the plan's sponsor able to adjust the plan's design (that is, benefit levels), if needed?
Underlying plan methods and assumptions	• Are underlying actuarial assumptions reasonable, such as the plan's discount rate or assumptions for inflation and salary growth?
	• Do the sponsor's actuarial methods for determining the rapidity of prefunding (actuarial cost methods for assigning costs to time periods, amortization periods, and any asset smoothing methods) produce a responsible path toward funding the obligation?
	• Who ultimately determines a plan's methods and assumptions?
	• Are those making these decisions doing so with sound professional judgment?
Managing risk	• Is a plan's investment portfolio properly positioned to balance risk and returns?
	• Has a risk evaluation, management, and reporting framework been identified to help manage plan risk?
	• Has the risk analysis and asset allocation decision taken into account relevant risk factors, such as the size of the sponsor's plans relative to the size of the plan sponsor's tax base, budget, or other measure of economic resources?
	• Do the plan's benefit formulas or governance processes subject the plan sponsor to the risk of significant increases in benefit promises?

Source: GAO analysis.

As illustrated in figure 3, an analysis of historical Census Bureau data on state and local government pensions shows that the ratio of fund assets to annual expenditures fell during the stock market downturn related to the oil crisis of the early 1970s, but eventually recovered and reached its peak in 2000, driven by strong investment results throughout the 1990s. Since that peak, both the market downturn in the early 2000s and sustained economic weakness beginning in 2008 drove the ratio of sector-wide assets relative to expenditures lower. Overall, these data show that the aggregate ratio of fund assets to annual expenditures, as of 2009, is lower, but in line with historical norms dating back to 1957.

Figure 3: Historical Trends in the Financial Condition of State and Local Government Pension Plans—Aggregate Ratio of Market Assets to Total Expenditures, 1957–2009

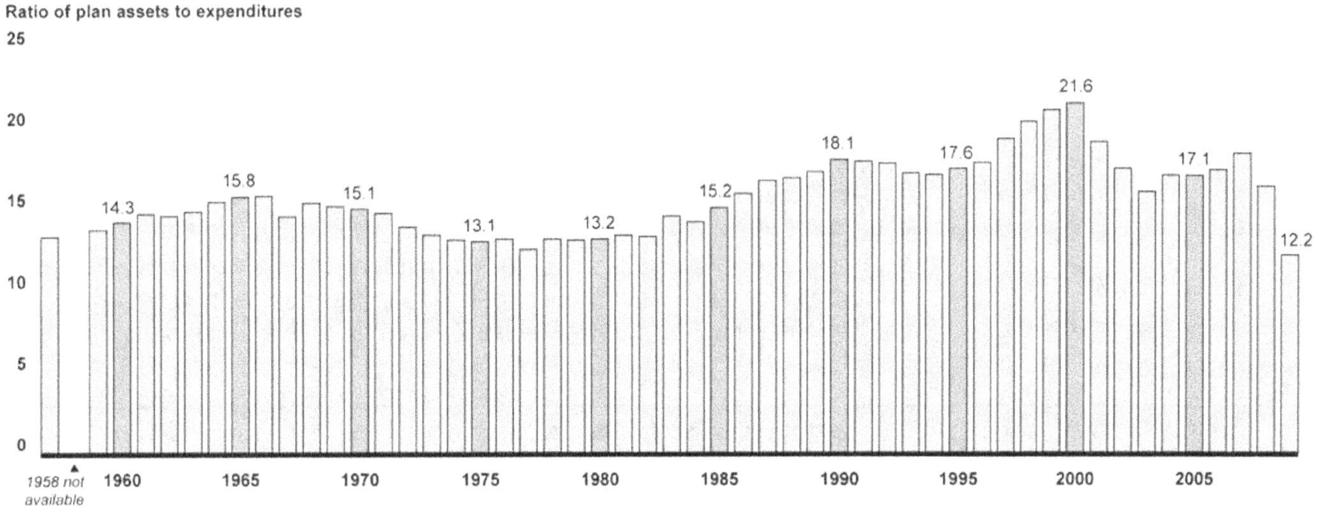

Ratio of plan assets to expenditures

Source: GAO analysis of nationwide Census data on state and local government pension plans

At the same time, data on individual plans indicate that this measure can vary considerably across plans. As illustrated in figure 4, data on large plans for fiscal year 2009 show that their fund assets relative to annual expenditures varied widely, with ratios ranging from less than 5 to greater than 20.

Figure 4: Variability in Large Plans' Ratios of Assets to Annual Expenditures, Fiscal Year 2009

Ratio of assets to expenditures

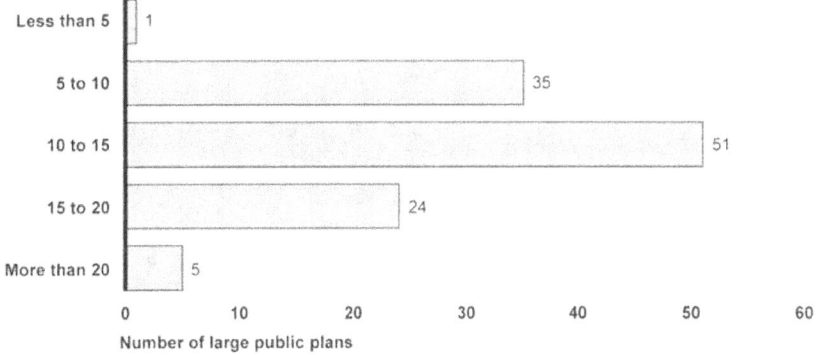

Source: GAO analysis of data on 116 large plans from the Center for Retirement Research at Boston College

GAO-12-322 State and Local Pensions

From the early years of prefunding of pension plans, sector-wide plan contributions outpaced plan expenditures, but by the early 1990s, expenditures began outpacing contributions.[16] This trend was predictable. As public plans matured, they began to have greater proportions of retirees to active workers. As such, payments to retirees increased relative to plan contributions and, as a result, in more recent years, sector-wide expenditures have outpaced contributions.[17] Nevertheless, given the asset levels of most state and local government plans and the pace of expenditures relative to contributions, most plans can be expected to cover their commitments for the near future with their existing assets.[18] For example, even if these plans received no more contributions or investment returns, most large plans would not exhaust their assets for a decade or longer, since they hold assets at least 10 times their annual expenditures.

Plans Face a Growing Gap between Assets and Liabilities, Leading to Higher Contribution Requirements

While state and local pension plans have sufficient assets to meet their obligations in the near future, an examination of actuarially determined funded ratios among large plans shows a growing gap between their

---

[16]This trend is consistent with actuarial practices of pension plans that have increasing proportions of retirees (that is, maturing plans).

[17]Whether pension funds grow or diminish depends on whether positive investment returns and contributions stay ahead of pension fund expenditures.

[18]A study by the Center for Retirement Research at Boston College analyzing plan assets relative to benefit payments and projecting these figures forward, assuming investment return rates of 6 and 8 percent respectively, showed that most large plans have enough prefunded resources to cover their benefit payments for at least 30 years, with a few notable exceptions. Plans included in this study were chosen from the largest plans from each state as well as a judgmental sample of locally administered plans. The study was based upon 2009 data that did not reflect investment return gains over 2010 or recent state and local government efforts to increase employee contributions and reduce benefits for new employees, See Alicia H. Munnell, Jean-Pierre Aubry, Josh Hurwitz, and Laura Quinby, *Can State and Local Pensions Muddle Through?*(March 2011). Also, just prior to the economic crisis, we reported that most state and local government pension plans had enough invested resources to keep up with benefits they were scheduled to pay for several decades. See GAO, *State and Local Government Retiree Benefits: Current Funded Status of Pension and Health Benefits*, GAO-08-223 (Washington, D.C.: Jan. 29, 2008). There have been other studies projecting the longevity of state and local pension plans; notably a study by Joshua Rauh, see Joshua D. Rauh, *Are State Public Pensions Sustainable? Why the Federal Government Should Worry About State Pension Liabilities*, (May 15, 2010). The study projected some notably early fund exhaustion dates, including some funds running out of money this decade. However, the study was based on the assumption that benefits earned to date would only be financed out of current plan assets and not from any future contributions. The projected exhaustion dates are thus not realistic estimates of when the funds might actually run out of money.

assets and liabilities.[19] This ratio is important since, on a plan-by-plan basis, a plan's funded ratio shows the plan's funding progress and is part of the basis for determining contribution levels necessary for fund sustainability.[20] As a result of recent market declines and other reasons—such as sponsors' failure to keep pace with their actuarially required contributions and benefit increases during the early 2000s—funded ratios have trended lower. Data compiled on large plans indicate that the funded ratios for these plans, in aggregate, have fallen over the past decade from over 100 percent in fiscal year 2001 to 75.6 percent in fiscal year 2010.[21] (See fig. 5.)

---

[19]The funded ratio is calculated by dividing plan actuarial assets by plan actuarial liabilities. See appendix II for additional information on actuarial methods and measures.

[20]Current GASB standards include a measure known as the annual required contribution, or ARC, which is not necessarily the same amount as the contribution actually made by the employer to the plan. Conceptually, the ARC is an amount that would cover the employer's share of costs attributable to the current year of employee service (the "normal cost"), plus an amount to eliminate the plan's unfunded liability over an amortization period, all determined in accordance with an actuarially sound funding method selected for the plan (of which there are multiple choices). The accounting cost—that is, the cost for the year recognized in the employer's financial statements—is based on this ARC. In this sense, the accounting is based on the stated funding method selected by the employer. But the employer may or may not actually contribute the ARC in any given year, so that the accounting cost may differ from the funding cost. See appendix II for information on proposed changes to GASB standards.

[21]Analyzing the aggregate level of large plans minimizes the difficulties in making comparisons across plans with actuarially based data, since these data include the same group of plans over time. Most plans keep their key actuarial methods fairly steady over time, with some significant exceptions. For example, any given plan will typically use a similar cost method, smoothing, and amortization period over time.

Figure 5: Aggregate Funding Ratio: Trend Data for Large State and Local Government Pension Plans, Fiscal Years 2001–2010

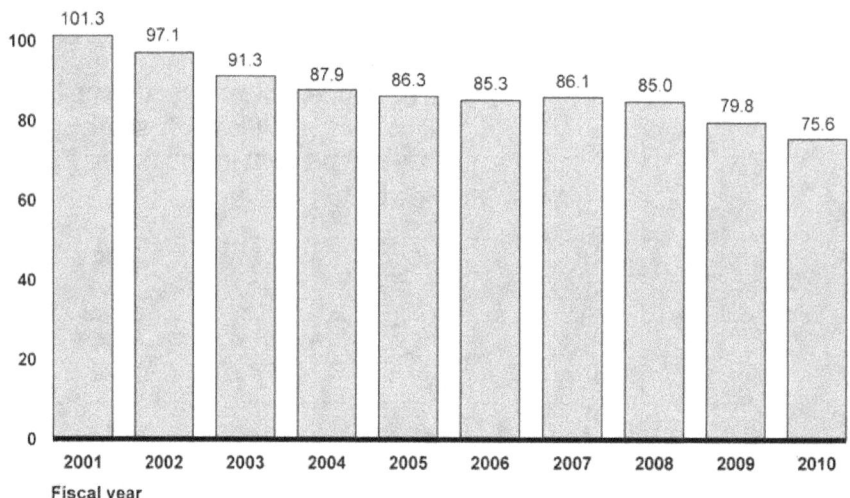

Aggregate funding ratio (in percent)

Source: GAO analysis of data on large plans from the National Association of State Retirement Administrators' Public Fund Survey and the Center for Retirement Research at Boston College.

Note: The number of large plans included in the analysis ranged from 119 to 126 plans.

Growing Gap between Actuarial Assets and Liabilities

Several factors have contributed to the growing gap between plans' actuarial assets and liabilities. For example, large pension funds generally assumed investment returns ranging from 6 to 9 percent throughout the 2000s, including assuming returns of approximately 8 percent, on average, in 2009, despite the declines in the stock market during this time.[22] Pension portfolios maintain other assets beside equities; however, gains in these other asset classes did not make up the amounts lost by negative equity performance over this period.[23] It is important to note that the period from 2008 to 2009 was an extraordinary low period for returns on investments in the financial history of the United States.

---

[22]Plans typically perform "experience studies" as one factor to guide them in making adjustments to their underlying actuarial assumptions such as adjusting expected employee salary levels or retiree life expectancies.

[23]See National Association of State Retirement Administrators, *Public Fund Survey Summary of Findings for FY2009*, (November 2010).

Benefit increases were another important reason for the growing gap between assets and liabilities over the past decade. These increases were enacted early in the decade when the funded status of plans was strong. For example, 11 states increased pension benefits in 2001 according to reports from the National Conference of State Legislatures.[24] Among the sites included in our review, Pennsylvania enacted legislation in 2001 that increased the pension benefit multiplier from 2 to 2.5 percent—an increase of 25 percent.[25] This higher benefit formula applied to both new and currently employed pension plan members (covering state employees and local public school employees). This was also the case in California and Colorado where pension benefit increases in the late 1990s and early in the 2000s helped drive liabilities higher.

Actuarially Determined Contribution Rates Trending Higher

Lower funded ratios generally mean higher annual contribution rates are necessary to help sustain pension plans. Thus, as funded ratios trended lower over the past decade, sponsor contribution rates trended higher. For example, from 2002 to 2009, the median government sponsor contribution rates among large plans rose as a percentage of payroll, while employee contribution levels remained the same through this same period (see table 3).

Table 3: Median Contribution Rates for Large Plans as a Percentage of Payroll

		2002	2009
Plans **not** participating in Social Security	Employer	10.3%	12.7%
	Employee	8	8
Plans participating in Social Security	Employer	6	9.4
	Employee	5%	5%

Source: National Association of State Retirement Administrators.

In spite of budget pressures through the 2007-2009 recession, most government sponsors of large plans continued to contribute about the same percentage of their annual required contribution (ARC) levels

---

[24]See Ronald Snell, NCSL, *Pensions and Retirement Plan Enactments in 2001 State Legislatures (2001)*.

[25]Soon after Pennsylvania increased benefits, the state also changed its actuarial methods to amortize gains more quickly than losses, effectively suppressing the employer contribution rate over the subsequent 10-year period, according to plan officials.

determined to be needed to help sustain their fund assets.[26] From 2005 until 2009, just under two-thirds of large plan sponsors continued to pay at least 90 percent of their ARC payments.[27] However, the gap in dollars between what large plans would have received, in aggregate, if they received their full ARC payments is significant. For example, in 2009, large plans sponsors contributed approximately $63.9 billion in aggregate, $10.7 billion less than if they had made their full ARC payments.

In addition, the distribution of plan sponsor contribution levels in 2010, illustrated in figure 6, shows that about half the sponsors of large plans contributed their full 100 percent or more of ARC payments, while others contributed much less.

Figure 6: Distribution of Percentage of ARC Paid for Large Plans, Fiscal Year 2010

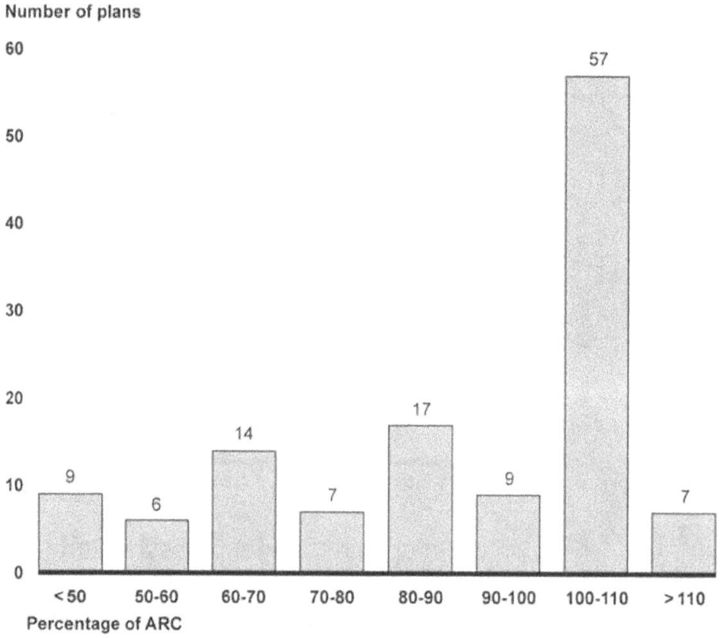

Source: GAO analysis of data from the Public Plans Database of the Center for Retirement Research at Boston College.

[26]A government sponsor may provide a lower percentage of the ARC from one year to the next, yet its contribution, in dollars, may be higher than the previous year's amount. This is significant from a budgeting perspective because of the year-to-year increase.

[27]This level had fallen since 2001, when 9 of every 10 large plan sponsors were paying at least 90 percent of their ARCs.

GAO-12-322 State and Local Pensions

Going forward, among the eight selected states and eight selected local jurisdictions we reviewed, several officials told us that they expected significant increases in their employer contribution rates as a percentage of payroll. For instance, officials from the Employees' Retirement System of Georgia expect their contribution rates to nearly double over the next 5 years (from 10.5 to 20 percent of payroll) to help maintain a sustainable path for their defined benefit plans. Officials from the Utah Retirement Systems expect rates to increase from approximately 13 to 20 percent of payroll.

Plans Are Vulnerable to Pressures on State and Local Budgets

Fiscal pressures on state and local governments' budgets add to the challenges faced by plan sponsors and their ability to make adequate contributions to their pension plans. The economic downturn and slow recovery led to budget shortfalls in the state and local sectors because of declining tax revenues and increased spending on economic safety net programs such as health care and social services. According to survey data from the National Association of State Budget Officers (NASBO), from fiscal years 2009 through 2011, states reported solving nearly $230 billion in gaps between projected spending and revenue levels.[28] Local governments have also struggled with their budgets. For example, the National League of Cities reported that if all city budgets were totaled together, they would likely face a combined estimated shortfall of anywhere from $56 billion to $83 billion from 2010 to 2012.[29]

As a result, higher pension contributions have been needed at the same time state and local governments have faced added pressures to balance their budgets. Even in normal economic times, state and local governments seek consistency in program spending areas, meaning that large year-to-year increases in pension contribution levels can strain

---

[28]NASBO, *Fiscal Survey of States: Spring 2011* (Washington, D.C.: 2011). In addition, NASBO notes that one of the clearest signs of fiscal stress is the need for states to make midyear budget cuts to help balance their budgets. Survey responses indicate that 43 states made such reductions in fiscal year 2009, and 39 states did so in fiscal year 2010.

[29]As an indication of extreme fiscal stress among local governments, a small number have filed for bankruptcy: 4 filed in 2008, 10 in 2009, 6 in 2010, and 4 as of June 2011. Since 1937, when the municipal bankruptcy code was instituted, there have been 624 filings as of June 30, 2011, according to an expert's analysis of municipal bankruptcy filings. See James E. Spiotto, "The Myth and Reality of State and Local Governments Debt Financing in the U.S.A. in Times of Financial Emergency," (July 25, 2011). Available on the U.S. Securities and Exchange Commission website.

budgets. Since some of these governments are subject to balanced budget requirements, annual pension contributions, which averaged around 4 percent of state and local budgets in fiscal year 2008, must compete with other pressing needs, even though pension costs are obligations that governments must eventually pay.[30]

Although tax revenues are slowly recovering to pre-2008 levels, going forward, long-term budget issues will likely continue to stress state and local governments and their ability to fund their pension programs. GAO has reported that state and local governments face fiscal challenges that will grow over time, and with current policies in place, the sector's fiscal health is projected to decline steadily through 2060.[31] The primary factor driving this decline is the projected growth in health-related costs. For example, GAO simulations show that the sector's health-related costs will be about 3.7 percent of gross domestic product in 2010, but grow to 8.3 percent by 2060.[32] These fiscal pressures, combined with growing pension contribution rates, have spurred many states and localities to take action to reduce pension costs and improve the future sustainability of their plans.

States and Localities Have Made Changes to Reduce Costs and Improve Plan Sustainability

States and localities have implemented various changes to their pension systems since the 2008 economic downturn—changes that, according to officials, were intended to help manage costs and improve plan

---

[30]Provisions in state constitutions, statutes, or recognized legal protections under common law often protect pensions from being eliminated or diminished for current or retired members. In a few rare exceptions, some jurisdictions have avoided paying promised benefits. This can happen in cases of government bankruptcy or when legislative changes to reduce benefits are made retroactively and survive any legal challenges.

[31]GAO, *State and Local Governments' Fiscal Outlook: April 2011 Update,* GAO-11-495SP (Washington, D.C.: Apr. 6, 2011).

[32]To provide more flexibility in addressing the growing cost of government employee' retiree health care, state and local jurisdictions have begun to prefund these costs. With prefunding, governments can reduce the unfunded liability reported in their financial statements, take advantage of the compounding effects of investment returns on plan assets, and provide greater benefit stability for employees and retirees. In addition, by setting aside funds for this purpose in advance, government contributions can be reduced when fiscal pressures are great. However, prefunding retiree health benefits requires higher contributions in the short term than pay-as-you-go financing requires. For further discussion of this topic, see GAO, *State and Local Government Retiree Health Benefits: Liabilities Are Largely Unfunded, but Some Governments Are Taking Action,* GAO-10-61, (Washington, D.C.: Nov. 30, 2009).

sustainability long term (see fig. 7). Based on our tabulation of state legislative changes reported annually by NCSL, we found that the majority of states have modified their existing defined benefit systems to reduce member benefits, lowering future liabilities. Half of states have increased required member (that is, employee) contributions, shifting costs to employees. Only a few states have adopted primary plans with defined contribution components, which reduce plan sponsors' investment risk by shifting it to employees. Some states and localities have also taken action to lower pension contributions in the short term by changing actuarial methods, and a few have issued pension bonds to finance their contributions or to lower their costs by reducing the gap between plan assets and liabilities. In general, we found that states and localities often package several of these different pension changes together. These packaged changes can have varying effects on employer contributions, plan sustainability, and employees' retirement security.[33]

Figure 7: Notable Changes to State-Sponsored Pension Plans, January 2008–June 2011

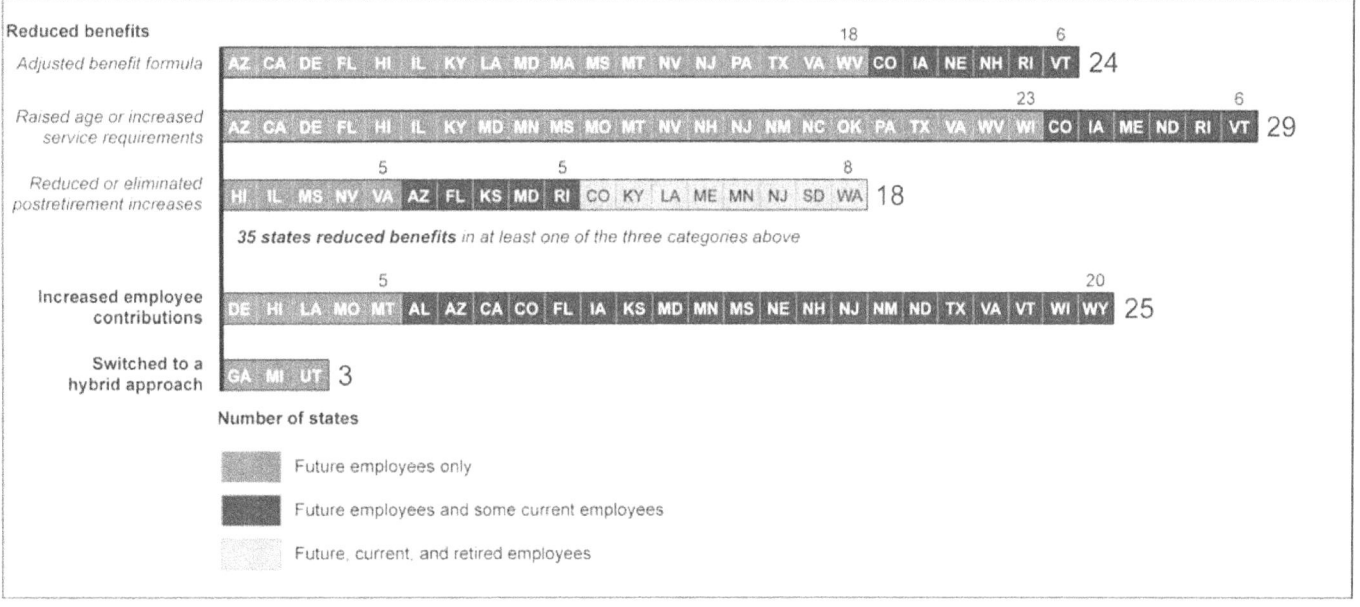

Source: GAO analysis of annual NCSL reports.

---

[33]See appendix I for a summary of the recent pension changes implemented in the eight states and eight localities we reviewed.

GAO-12-322 State and Local Pensions

Majority of States Have Reduced Benefits since 2008, Reducing Future Liabilities

Since the economic downturn in 2008, 35 states have modified at least one state-sponsored defined benefit system to reduce member benefits and lower future pension liabilities, according to our analysis of NCSL annual reports on recent pension legislation.[34] States and localities have used various strategies to reduce benefits for plan participants, such as adjusting the benefit formula, raising eligibility requirements, and limiting postretirement benefit increases:

- **Adjusting pension benefit formula.** Since 2008, 24 states have adjusted the defined benefit formulas to reduce benefits by expanding the time period for calculating final average salary or lowering the percentage of final average salary multiplied by years of service for determining benefits.[35] For example, California recently lowered the benefit multiplier for new state safety employees, many of whom are not covered by Social Security, from 2.5 to 2 percent. In addition, two localities we reviewed made similar changes. For example, Denver, Colorado, increased the period used for calculating final average salary from 3 to 5 years for new members of the Denver Employees Retirement Plan.

- **Raising eligibility requirements.** Since 2008, 29 states have increased retirement age or vesting requirements for plan participants.[36] For example, Missouri raised the normal retirement age for general employees from 62 to 67 and lengthened the vesting period from 5 to 10 years for new members of the State Employees' Retirement System and the Missouri Department of Transportation and Highway Patrol Employees' Retirement System. In addition, two localities we reviewed made similar changes. For example, the normal retirement age for new members of the Policemen's Annuity and Benefit Fund of Chicago was raised from 50 to 55 years.

- **Limiting postretirement benefits.** Since 2008, 18 states have reduced or eliminated annual postretirement cost-of-living adjustments (COLA). Some states have even applied these changes

---

[34]This analysis is based on our review of annual NCSL reports for the years 2008-2010 and a 2011 report that covered changes adopted by June of that year.

[35]Expanding the time period for calculating final average salaries generally reduces pension benefits by averaging in lower employee salaries.

[36]The vesting period is the employees' required years of service before they earn the right to future pension benefits.

to current retirees. In the case of Colorado, the state recently reduced postretirement COLAs for future, current, and retired members. According to plan documents, most plan members, who are not covered by Social Security, had previously been guaranteed an annual postretirement COLA of 3.5 percent, but the recent legislation eliminated the COLA for 2010 and capped future COLAs at 2 percent.[37]

The majority of these benefit changes have been limited to new employees, slowing the future growth of pension liabilities, but usually not significantly reducing systems' existing unfunded liabilities, which are based on the benefits promised to current employees and retirees.[38] As we have reported previously, provisions in state constitutions, statutes, or recognized legal protections under common law often protect pensions from being eliminated or diminished for current or retired members.[39] Thus, some state and local governments change benefits by creating a new tier or plan that applies to new employees hired only after the date of the change, and sometimes also to newer employees who are not yet vested. It takes time for these new employees with less expensive pension benefits to become a significant portion of the workforce, delaying for a decade or more any significant reductions in plan liabilities.[40] Over the long term, however, these benefit reductions can

---

[37]Prior to the 2010 legislation, the amount of postretirement COLAs depended on when employees joined the system, according to plan documents. The COLA amount was 3.5 percent for members who joined on or before June 30, 2005, and the lower of 3 percent or the Consumer Price Index for Urban Wage Earners and Clerical Workers (CPI-W) for members who joined on or after July 1, 2005. The 2010 legislation lowered the COLA for all future, current, and retired members. For members who joined before January 1, 2007, the COLA was reduced to 2 percent unless the plan has a negative investment return year, in which case the COLA will be the lesser of 2 percent or the CPI-W for the next three years. A separate reserve fund was created for members who joined on or after January 1, 2007. For these members, the COLA will be the lesser of 2 percent or the CPI-W as long as payments do not exceed 10 percent of the COLA reserve fund. The legislation also allows for the maximum COLA to be increased when the plan's overall funded status is at or above 103 percent and lowered if it subsequently drops below 90 percent.

[38]As discussed later, Illinois took the more unusual step of taking advance credit for benefit reductions that apply only to new employees.

[39]GAO, *State and Local Government Retiree Benefits: Current Status of Benefit Structures, Protections, and Fiscal Outlook for Funding Future Costs*, GAO-07-1156 (Washington, D.C.: Sept. 24, 2007).

[40]Employers with higher rates of employee turnover will recognize savings from pension benefit reductions sooner than those employers with less employee turnover.

reduce pension liabilities and consequently lower actuarially required sponsor contributions. From the employee perspective, these changes can mean that those in the new tier or plan will realize lower future benefits than their coworkers who continue to participate in the old plan. This could affect employee recruitment and retention over the long term, but some pension officials we spoke with expected any short-term impacts to be minimal.

Among the pension plans included in our review, we found that six states and two localities had reduced the benefits in some of their largest defined benefit plans. For example, in 2011, Denver, Colorado, reduced retirement benefits for new members of the Denver Employees Retirement Plan hired after July 1, 2011. Denver reversed previous benefit enhancements enacted over prior decades by increasing the period used for calculating final average salary (the basis for benefit calculations) and raising the minimum retirement age from 55 to 60, among other changes. Over the next 30 years, these changes are expected to reduce the city's pension contributions by 1.65 percent of payroll. According to plan documents, the changes enacted are expected to reduce pension benefits for new employees and will require some members to work longer to receive full pension benefits. Nevertheless, city officials do not expect any of the recent changes to significantly affect employee recruitment and retention.

Half the States Have Raised Member Contributions, Shifting Costs to Plan Members

Twenty-five states have taken action since 2008 to increase member contributions, shifting pension costs to employees, according to NCSL reports. States generally have more leeway to adjust member contribution rates as compared with pension benefits for existing members. As a result, more states have increased contributions for some active employees rather than limiting the increases to future employees. Some states are also requiring members to contribute to their pensions for the first time. Among the states we reviewed, Virginia and Missouri recently required some new plan members to contribute to the retirement plan (5 percent in Virginia and 4 percent in Missouri), whereas members did not previously contribute.

Increases in member contributions reduce the actuarially required amounts plan sponsors need to contribute to their pension systems. As a result, these changes often do not affect the amount of revenue flowing into pension systems, but rather represent a shifting of pension cost from employers to plan members. Member contributions are a relatively stable source of pension revenue, since they are less susceptible to market conditions than investment returns, and less susceptible to budgetary and political pressures than employer contributions. However, member contributions are susceptible to declines in the size of the workforce and are often refunded to employees if they separate from their employer before becoming eligible to receive benefits.

Among the jurisdictions included in our review, we found that four states and one locality had increased the member contributions in some of their largest defined benefit plans. For example, in the case of Norfolk, Virginia, the city began requiring new members to contribute 5 percent to the Employees' Retirement System in 2010, whereas current members do not contribute. As a result of this change, the city's employer contributions will decline as more contributing members join the system. City officials said that new employees had already contributed over $140,000 to the system in the first year. This increase in member contributions will reduce employee compensation and could affect recruitment and retention, particularly since the change will be immediately reflected in lower paychecks. However, city officials did not expect the changes to have a significant impact on employee recruitment and retention, since the Virginia Retirement System had recently implemented similar changes for state employees.

Three States Recently Adopted Hybrid Approaches, Reducing Risk for Plan Sponsors

Although a majority of states have continued to use traditional defined benefit plans as their primary pension system, our analysis of NCSL annual reports on recent pension legislation found that, since 2008, three states—Georgia, Michigan,[41] and Utah—have implemented hybrid approaches as primary plans for large groups of employees,[42] shifting

---

[41]Michigan has operated a defined contribution plan for general employees since 1997, but adopted a new hybrid system for public school employees in 2010.

[42]Prior to 2008, three states, Alaska, Indiana, and Oregon, and the District of Columbia had already adopted defined contribution or hybrid approaches as their primary plans for general public employees. Indiana has operated a hybrid system since 1997, but adopted a defined contribution option for new employees in 2011. In addition, Nebraska maintains a cash balance defined benefit plan as its primary plan. Although still providing defined benefit plans as their primary plans for general state employees, some states also offer defined contribution plans or hybrid approaches as optional alternatives to their primary plans. These states include Colorado, Florida, Montana, Ohio, South Carolina, and Washington.

some investment risk to new employees.[43] Two of the eight localities we reviewed have also switched to hybrid approaches since 2008: Cobb County, Georgia, and Bountiful, Utah (which participates in Utah's state-administered retirement system). Unlike in a defined benefit plan, which provides benefits based on a set formula,[44] in a defined contribution component of a hybrid approach, the key determinants of the benefit amount are the employee's and employer's contribution rates, and the rate of return achieved on the amounts contributed to an individual's account over time.

Defined contribution and hybrid approaches reduce the impact of market volatility on plan funding and employer contributions, but are riskier for plan members. Whereas under a defined benefit system, employer contributions generally rise and fall depending in part on investment returns, plan sponsors of a defined contribution system contribute a set amount regardless of investment returns. This reduces the risk facing the pension system as well as the state or locality sponsoring the plan. However, switching to a defined contribution plan can involve additional short-term costs for plan sponsors, since contributions from new employees go toward their own private accounts rather than paying off existing unfunded liabilities of the defined benefit plan once it is closed to new employees. From the member's perspective, building up retirement savings in defined contribution plans rests on factors that are, to some degree, outside of the control of the individual worker. Most notable among these is the market return on plan assets, which, among other factors, determines future retirement benefits. On the one hand, this exposure to market risk increases members' financial uncertainty, since retirement benefits rise and fall based on investment returns. On the other hand, defined contribution plans are often viewed as more portable than defined benefit plans, as employees own their accounts individually and can generally take their balances with them—including both member and

---

[43]In this report we use the term "hybrid approach" to refer to public pension systems that combine defined benefit and defined contribution components. In the private sector, a hybrid plan most often refers to a cash balance plan, which is legally a defined benefit plan that expresses benefits as a hypothetical individual account balance that is based on pay credits (percentage of salary or compensation) and interest credits. For additional information on private sector cash balance plans, see GAO, *Private Pensions: Information on Cash Balance Pension Plans*, GAO-06-42 (Washington, D.C.: Nov. 3, 2005).

[44]In a public sector defined benefit plan, the amount of the benefit is determined by a formula typically based on the retiree's years of service and final average salary.

employer contributions—when they leave government employment, as long as they are vested. In contrast, employees in defined benefit plans can generally take their member contributions, if any, with them if they leave government employment, but not the employer's contributions. [45]

In the case of Georgia, the state replaced its defined benefit plan with a hybrid approach for all new employees hired after January 1, 2009. This new hybrid approach is composed of a smaller defined benefit relative to the previous plan (1 percent of highest average salary multiplied by years of service compared with 2 percent previously) and automatic enrollment in the state's 401(k) plan with the state matching up to 3 percent of the employee's contributions.[46] Plan officials said it is difficult to calculate how much the state will save as a result of the change, but it is expected to be financially advantageous for the state in the long run. In 2011, employer contributions for the defined benefit portion of the hybrid approach were 6.54 percent of payroll, compared with 10.41 percent for employees covered under the old plan. However, since the changes are limited to new employees, it will take time for the state to realize significant savings from the change. According to plan officials, one of the motivating factors behind the switch to the hybrid approach was the desire to attract new employees to the state by providing them with more portable retirement benefits that mirrored those in the private sector. However, as is common with defined contribution plans in the private sector, some participants in the hybrid approach may not be saving enough for a secure retirement. As of December 31, 2011, 80 percent of employees participating in the

---

[45]Once an employee is vested, both defined contribution and defined benefit plans could be regarded as "portable." In the case of a defined benefit plan, the departing employee takes with him or her the right to a future benefit, wherever he or she goes. However, the benefit formulas of defined benefit plans are often weighted toward employees that retire after many years of service with a single employer, so workers changing jobs may incur future lifetime benefit losses. The perception of defined contribution plans as more portable reflects the greater liquidity and employee discretion over the management of these benefits, such as the ability to cash them out upon leaving employment, or to roll them over into another plan or an individual retirement account. For additional information, see GAO, *Private Pensions: Alternative Approaches Could Address Retirement Risks Faced by Workers but Pose Trade-offs*, GAO-09-642 (Washington D.C.: July 24, 2009).

[46]A 401(k) plan is a type of defined contribution plan that permits employees to defer a portion of their pay to a qualified tax-deferred plan. State and local government defined contribution plans are typically 457(b) plans. The Tax Reform Act of 1986 prohibited state and local governments from establishing any new 401(k) plans after May 6, 1986, but existing plans were allowed to continue. Pub. L. No. 99-514, § 1116(b)(3), 100 Stat. 2085, 2455.

401(k) component of the hybrid approach were contributing only the default 1 percent, according to plan officials. At this level, employees may struggle to build adequate retirement savings. Plan officials said they have tried to encourage members to contribute more to their 401(k) plans, but these efforts have not been successful.

Some States and Localities Have Adjusted Pension Funding Practices, Potentially Increasing Future Costs

To address rising actuarially required pension contribution levels and budget pressures, some states and localities have taken actions to limit employer contributions in the short term or refinance their contributions.[47] These strategies included changing actuarial methods or issuing pension bonds to supplement other sources of financing for pension plans. Such strategies help plan sponsors manage their contributions in the near term, but may increase their future costs. Fewer nationwide data are available on the use of these strategies; however, we were able to document their use across several of our selected pension plans.[48]

Adjusting Actuarial Methods

Some state and local governments have limited or deferred their pension contributions in the short term by making actuarial changes. It is difficult to determine the recent prevalence of these changes nationwide; however, five of the eight states and one of the localities we reviewed had implemented actuarial changes to reduce their pension contributions since 2008.[49] The changes included expanding amortization periods (the number of years allotted to pay off unfunded liabilities) and adjusting smoothing techniques (methods for reducing the effect of market volatility

---

[47]State and local plan sponsors can also address their pension finance challenges by adjusting their investment policy, particularly plan asset allocation, which is the third key mechanism, besides benefit policy and funding policy, that plan sponsors have in attempting to manage the amount, riskiness, and sustainability of their pension costs. A less risky asset allocation can raise estimated costs but also make them less volatile; a more risky allocation can lower estimated costs but at the price of greater risk. We have previously reported that state and local plans have gradually changed their asset portfolios over many years by increasing their allocations in higher-risk investments partly in pursuit of higher returns. See GAO, *State and Local Government Pension Plans: Governance Practices and Long-Term Investment Strategies Have Evolved Gradually as Plans Take On Increased Investment Risk*, GAO-10-754, (Washington, D.C.: Aug. 24, 2010).

[48]Since implementation of actuarial changes sometimes does not require a legislative change, use of such strategies is not reflected in the NCSL annual reports of state legislative changes. As a result, our analysis of such changes is based on reviews of our selected states and localities rather than NCSL reports.

[49]In the states we reviewed, actuarial changes were implemented either by state legislation or by the pension plan boards.

on pension contributions by averaging asset values over multiple years).[50] For example, Utah reported that it increased the amortization for the state's retirement system from 20 years to 25 years to extend the length of time for paying down unfunded pension liabilities.[51] Alternatively, Illinois reported that it recently required all Illinois state retirement systems to switch from a market valuation with no smoothing to a 5-year smoothing method for calculating actuarial assets and employer contributions to lessen the immediate impact of fiscal year 2009 investment losses on contributions.

Capping or Postponing Employer Contributions

Some state and local governments, while not formally changing their underlying actuarial methods, have simply deferred or capped their pension contributions. Two states and one locality we reviewed limited contributions in the short term by capping increases in employer contributions or by simply postponing otherwise scheduled contributions. Capping increases in contributions allowed these states and this locality to temporarily suppress the increases that would otherwise have been required given 2008 investment losses and other factors. In the case of the Pennsylvania, the state addressed an expected 19 percent increase in actuarially required contributions to the State Employees' Retirement System by capping annual increases at 3 percent for 2012, 3.5 percent for 2013, and 4.5 percent thereafter. Similarly, the Illinois Municipal Retirement Fund allowed local plan sponsors to cap contribution increases at 10 percent starting in 2010.

Although adjusting plan funding produced some short-term savings for state and local budgets, it also increased the unfunded liabilities of the pension system and will necessitate larger contributions in the future. In the case of Philadelphia, the city used its authority under state law to partially defer pension payments by $150 million in fiscal year 2010 and $90 million in 2011. While these deferrals helped the city reduce its contributions in the short term, state law requires that the money be

---

[50]Other actuarial changes, such as reducing the assumed rate of investment returns, can increase actuarially required pension contributions.

[51]Utah moved from an open 20-year amortization period (meaning that the amortization was frozen at 20 years) to a closed 25-year amortization period (meaning that the amortization period will decrease annually by one year). As a result, Utah is currently at a 23 year amortization period, and the period will continue to decrease annually unless its board takes action to change the amortization policy.

repaid with interest by fiscal year 2014. The city has adopted a temporary 1 percent increase in the sales tax to help cover these future costs.[52]

Issuing Pension Obligation Bonds

Issuing pension obligation bonds (POB) is another funding strategy, although relatively few states and localities have used it, as it can expose plan sponsors to additional market risk. POBs are taxable general obligation bonds that provide a one-time cash infusion into the pension system. They convert a current pension obligation into a long-term, fixed obligation of the government issuing the bond. POBs are issued for generally one of two purposes: either to provide temporary budget relief by financing a plan sponsor's actuarially required contribution for a single year, or as part of a longer-term strategy for paying off a plan's unfunded liability. Using POBs to pay off all or a portion of a plan's unfunded liability potentially reduces future actuarially required pension contributions, but requires plan sponsors to make annual debt service payments on the POBs instead.[53]

We analyzed data on state and local government bond issuances nationwide and found that other than the states of Illinois and Connecticut, and the Chicago Transit Authority, most state and local governments have not issued sizable POBs over the past 6 years (see fig. 8). This type of pension funding has been limited, with only 25 or fewer POB issuances in each of the last 6 years. The total amount of POBs issued in a single year has not exceeded more than 1 percent of total assets in state and local pension plans.

---

[52]Philadelphia was not the only locality we reviewed that used a temporary tax increase to cover pension contributions. In 2009, Springfield, Missouri approved a 0.75 cent sales tax, all of which will go toward funding the city's Police Officers' and Firefighters' Retirement Fund.

[53]Issuing POBs can be a leveraging strategy, since funds are borrowed at a fixed interest rate and then invested in the stock market in an attempt to achieve a higher rate of return (arbitrage).

Figure 8: Pension Obligation Bond Issuances Nationwide, January 2006–June 2011

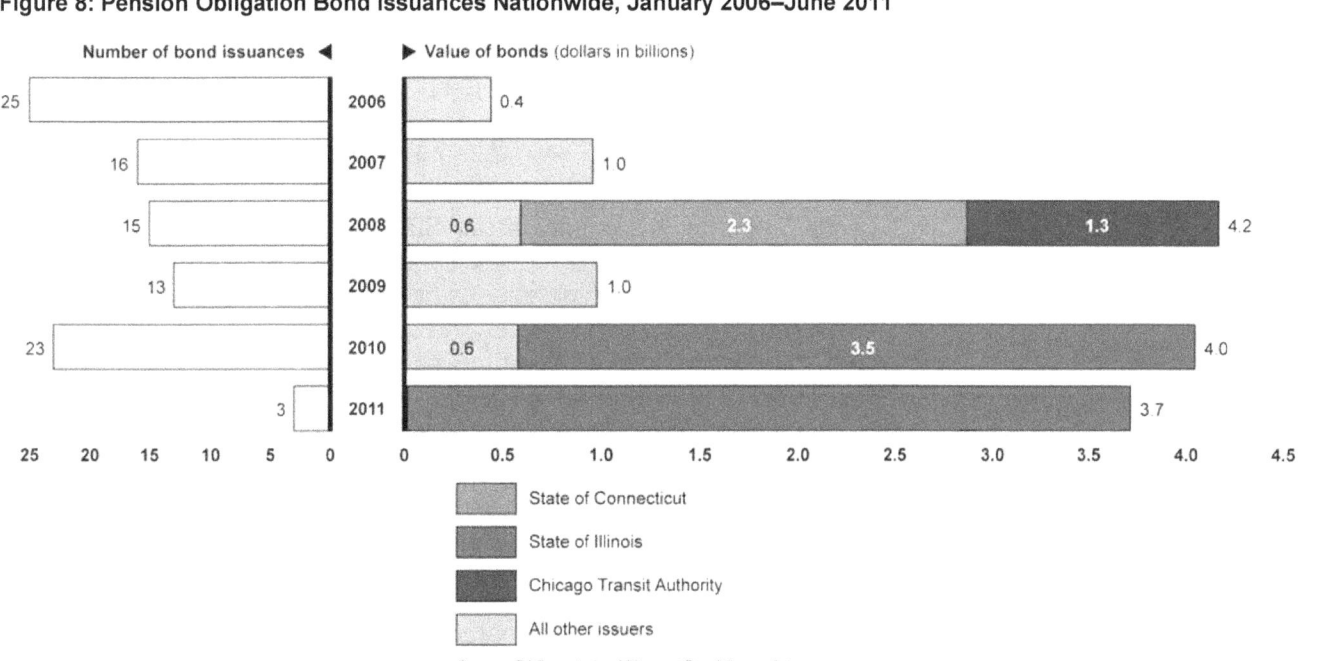

Source: GAO analysis of Mergent BondViewer data.

These transactions involve significant risks for government entities because investment returns on the bond proceeds can be volatile and lower than the interest rate on the bonds. In these cases, POBs can leave plan sponsors worse off than they were before, juggling debt service payments on the POBs in addition to their annual pension contributions. In a recent brief, the Center for State and Local Government Excellence reported that by mid-2009, most POBs issued since 1992 were a net drain on government revenues.[54] In light of these concerns, officials in

---

[54]Center for State and Local Government Excellence, *Issue Brief: Pension Obligation Bonds: Financial Crisis Exposes Risks* (Washington, D.C., January 2010).

Pennsylvania noted that the state had enacted legislation in 2010 prohibiting the use of POBs.[55]

Two of the pension systems included in our review—Illinois and Sonoma County, California—have issued POBs since 2008. Illinois, which is discussed at length below, has been the largest single issuer in recent years, issuing over $7 billion in POBs since 2010. In the case of Sonoma County, California, the county issued $289 million of POBs in 2010 with maturities ranging up to 19 years. County officials explained that the POBs were financially advantageous because they had an average interest rate of just under 6 percent, which is lower than the 8 percent expected return on the pension fund investments at the time the bonds were issued. The difference between the POB interest rates and the assumed rate of return is projected to save the county $93 million in contributions over the life of the bonds.[56] However, results could vary significantly. The POBs could increase the county's future expenses if actual investment returns fall below 6 percent. Over the prior 10-year period ending in 2010, the retirement system's average investment rate of return was 4.1 percent, but returns over the prior 20-year period have been significantly higher at 8.4 percent.

States and Localities Often Combine Strategies

States and localities often packaged multiple pension changes together. For example, our analysis of the NCSL reports revealed that 23 states have both increased employee contributions and reduced member benefits. Each change made, and the interplay among the changes, contributes to various impacts on plan sponsors, pension sustainability, and plan members. The following examples demonstrate some of the ways states have packaged these changes, and the varying impacts that are expected as a result.

---

[55]The provisions of Pennsylvania's pension reform legislation (Act 2010-120), enacted in November 2010, are summarized in Commonwealth of Pennsylvania State Employees' Retirement System, Comprehensive Annual Financial Report for the year ended December 31, 2010 (Harrisburg, PA: May 2011). The report describes the act's provisions for reducing benefits for future plan members and for changing funding methods, and notes that the act also prohibits the use of pension obligation bonds for funding liabilities. 24 Pa. C.S.A. § 8308 (2010).

[56]The county pension system subsequently lowered its assumed rate of return to 7.75 percent. This action, along with any future actuarial changes, would affect the expected savings from the POBs.

Reducing Benefits and Increasing Contributions for New Members

Missouri is an example of a state that packaged increases in member contributions with reductions in benefits to narrow the gap between plan assets and liabilities. For new general members of the Missouri State Employees Retirement System and the Missouri Department of Transportation and Highway Patrol Employees' Retirement System, the state increased the normal retirement age from 62 to 67, expanded the vesting period from 5 to 10 years, and required members to contribute 4 percent of pay to the pension system, although current members do not contribute. These changes are expected to lower the state's contributions to the system over the long run by more than 5 percent of payroll, but the initial savings are much smaller. In fiscal year 2012, the benefit and contribution changes are expected to reduce the state's contribution to its largest plan by less than 1 percent of payroll, since there will be only a small number of newly hired members in the system. However, by fiscal year 2018, employees covered under the reduced benefit structure are expected to account for over half of payroll, further reducing the state's annual contributions. Plan officials said these changes could pose issues for recruitment and retention, although the influence of retirement plan details will vary based on individual circumstances. They also noted that the changes could affect employee morale, since new employees will have to work longer to qualify for benefits and the required pension contributions will reduce their compensation.

Combining Short-Term Funding Adjustments with Longer-Term Benefit Reductions

In the case of Pennsylvania, the state passed a package of pension changes in 2010 that offset a short-term funding cap with long-term benefit reductions to limit the impact on the plan's funded status. For the State Employees' Retirement System, the most significant funding change was a statutory cap on employer contribution rate increases. The legislation addressed an expected 19 percent increase in actuarially required contributions by capping any increases at 3 percent for fiscal year 2011/2012, 3.5 percent for fiscal year 2012/2013, and 4.5 percent thereafter. In the short term, the caps effectively reduced the state's expected contributions over the next 4 years by $2.5 billion. But in the long term, the caps, along with other actuarial changes, are expected to increase the state's pension contributions to the system by $7 billion over the next 32 years. To help offset the additional long-term costs, Pennsylvania enacted pension legislation calling for various benefit reductions for future employees. For example, the state reduced the benefit multiplier for future employees from 2.5 to 2 percent (with an option for members to maintain the 2.5 multiplier by paying a higher member contribution rate); increased the normal retirement age from 60 to 65; and expanded the vesting period from 5 to 10 years. These benefit reductions will reduce future liabilities and are expected to lower the state's pension costs by almost $8.5 billion over the next 32 years, for an estimated net savings of $1.5 billion over the cost of the caps and other funding adjustments. Both pension and budget officials said these changes will help the state better manage rising pension contributions in the short term, but the overall savings from the legislative package are relatively modest over the long term. Meanwhile, the changes will require new employees to work longer for lower benefits and will leave more employees with no benefit at all. Plan officials said it is too early to tell if this will affect employee recruitment and retention. [57]

Managing Funding through POBs, Actuarial Changes, and Benefit Reductions

In the case of Illinois, the state combined use of POBs, actuarial changes, and benefit reductions to manage the state's pension costs. The state issued $3.5 billion of POBs in 2010 and $3.7 billion in 2011 with maturities up to 8 years and used the proceeds to fund the state's annual contributions to various pension systems. An Illinois budget official explained that issuing the POBs helped the state avoid making additional spending cuts to other portions of the state's budget. Alternatively, given the state's budgetary challenges, some pension officials said that if the state had not issued the POBs, it is more likely that it would have not paid its full required pension contributions.

Use of POBs will be costly to Illinois, since the state will face annual debt service payments of about $1 billion over the next 9 years. However, the state increased individual and corporate taxes in 2010 and state budget officials told us the state plans to use the additional revenue to fund these debt service payments as well as other budgetary priorities. Whether the state's statutorily required contributions are funded through POBs or general revenue does not directly affect the financial condition of the pension system. However, some pension officials were concerned that the debt service payments on the POBs would reduce available funding for future pension contributions.

Illinois has also lowered employer contributions to the state's pension systems in the short term by adjusting actuarial methods. In 2009, the state required its pension systems to switch from a market value (no smoothing) to a 5-year smoothing method for calculating actuarial assets

---

[57]The expanded vesting requirement, from 5 years to 10, would mean that more employees would leave service with no benefit at all, except for a return of member contributions. In the private sector, 5-year vesting has been the standard for defined benefit plans since 1986.

and employer contributions. Plan officials explained that the change was intended to reduce the state's contributions and dampen the impact of fiscal year 2009 market losses for the short term. As a result of the change, the state's actuarially calculated contribution to the State Employees' Retirement System of Illinois was reduced by $100 million in the first year, according to plan officials. However, plan actuaries noted that this strategy only defers contributions when plan assets experience a loss, as they did in fiscal year 2009. Future contributions will be higher than they would have been previously once the fiscal year 2009 market losses are fully recognized.

In addition to the use of POBs and actuarial changes, Illinois also reduced benefits for new employees and applied the future savings to reduce employer contributions in the short term. For example, the state raised new employees' normal retirement age to 67, capped final average salaries used for pension purposes, and reduced annual COLAs.[58] According to plan officials, these changes are expected to reduce the State Employees' Retirement System's future liabilities by a third. State budget officials said the projected total estimated savings for the state over the next 35 years will be about $220 billion. Since the changes apply only to new employees, the savings will slowly accrue over the next 35 years. Nevertheless, the state took advanced credit for these future benefit reductions, further reducing contributions in the short term. According to plan actuaries, by taking this advance credit, the state also increased unfunded liabilities in the short term, adversely affecting its retirement systems.

Concluding Observations

State and local governments continue to experience the lingering effects of investment losses and budget pressures in the wake of the recent economic downturn. Although most large state and local government pension plans still maintain substantial assets, sufficient to cover their pension obligations for a decade or more, heightened concerns over the long-term sustainability of the plans has spurred many states and localities to implement a variety of reforms, including reductions in benefits and increases in member contributions.

---

[58]According to plan officials, capping salaries used for benefit calculations and for determining contributions decreases the anticipated amount of future payroll and employee contributions, which affects future state contributions.

Despite these efforts, continued vigilance is needed to help ensure that states and localities can continue to meet their pension obligations. Several factors will ultimately affect the sustainability of state and local pension plans over the long term. Important among them are whether government sponsors maintain adequate contributions toward these plans, and whether investment returns meet sponsors' long-term assumptions. Going forward, growing budget pressures will continue to challenge state and local governments' abilities to provide adequate contributions to help sustain their pension plans and ensure a secure retirement for current and future employees.

Agency Comments

We provided officials from the Internal Revenue Service and the Social Security Administration with a draft of this report. They provided technical comments that we incorporated, as appropriate. In addition, we provided officials from the states and cities we reviewed with portions of the draft report that addressed aspects of the pension funds in their jurisdictions. We incorporated their technical comments, as appropriate, as well.

We are sending copies of this report to relevant congressional committees, the Commissioners of the Internal Revenue Service and the Social Security Administration, and other interested parties. In addition, this report will be available at no charge on GAO's website at http://www.gao.gov.

If you have any questions concerning this report, please contact Barbara D. Bovbjerg at (202) 512-7215 or Stanley J. Czerwinski at (202) 512-6806. Contact points for our Office of Congressional Relations and Public Affairs may be found on the last page of this report. GAO staff who made major contributions to this report are listed in appendix III.

Barbara D. Bovbjerg
Managing Director, Education, Workforce,
   and Income Security Issues

Stanley J. Czerwinski
Director, Strategic Issues

Profiles of Selected State and Local Government Pensions

United States

Overview of nationwide state and local retirement systems (FY 2009)

Number of plans: 3,418

- State plans: 222
- Local plans: 3,196

Active members: 14,829,943

- State plans: 13,112,318
- Local plans: 1,717,625

Beneficiaries: 7,990,405

- State plans: 6,751,285
- Local plans: 1,239,120

Percentage of members covered by Social Security: 73

Assets (thousands): $2,465,959,589

- State plans: $2,029,509,728
- Local plans: $436,449,861

Contributions (thousands)

- Employees: $39,511,586
- State government: $35,509,035
- Local government:$50,611,000

Source: GAO analysis of most recent Census and Social Security data.

Note: Census categorizes plans as state or local based on their level of administration, not sponsorship.

Methodology

We reviewed a small judgmental sample of plans from eight states, and one locality within each of these states, that have implemented pension modifications since 2008. This judgmental sample was selected to provide examples of plans experiencing a range of financial conditions and types of strategies adopted by their sponsors. The profiles on the following pages are based on information from the U.S. Census Bureau, Social Security Administration, pension plan documents (including Comprehensive Annual Financial Reports (CAFR)), and interviews with state and local government officials. At each location, we interviewed budget officials and pension plan administrators, and obtained documents describing recent changes to their plans. The descriptions of recent pension reforms included here highlight notable changes given the scope of our review; they are not intended to provide a comprehensive list of every change implemented by each state or locality. We did not conduct an independent legal review of any state or local laws in compiling this appendix.

State and Local Jurisdictions Selected for Review

- California and Sonoma County
- Colorado and the City of Denver
- Georgia and Cobb County
- Illinois and the City of Chicago
- Missouri and the City of Springfield
- Pennsylvania and the City of Philadelphia
- Utah and the City of Bountiful
- Virginia and the City of Norfolk

Profiles of Selected State and Local Government Pensions

California and Sonoma County

California
Sonoma County

Number of plans: 62

- State plans: 5
- Local plans: 57

Active members: 1,767,618

- State plans: 1,396,440
- Local plans: 371,178

Beneficiaries: 1,017,122

- State plans: 779,637
- Local plans: 237,485

Percentage of members covered by Social Security: 44

Assets (thousands): $470,140,330

- State plans: $340,161,617
- Local plans: $129,978,713

Contributions (thousands)

- Employees: $18,217,580
- State government: $4,426,716
- Local government:$10,785,868

Source: GAO analysis of most recent Census and Social Security data.

Note: Census categorizes plans as state or local based on their level of administration, not sponsorship.

Selected state-sponsored plans

Plan basics	California Public Employees' Retirement System (CalPERS)	California State Teachers' Retirement System
As of June 30, 2011		
Active members	791,219	429,600
Beneficiaries	536,234	253,041
Members covered by Social Security?	Varies by plan	No
Net assets (thousands)	$241,761,791	$155,345,815
Contributions: Employees	$3,600,089	$2,355,909
(thousands) Employers	$7,465,397	$3,503,615*

Source: GAO analysis of most recent plan CAFRs.

*This also includes government contributions

Benefit reductions: The state reduced benefits for new members of CalPERS hired on or after January 15, 2011, including

- raising the normal retirement age from 55 to 60 for general state employees and from age 50 to 55 for members of the state highway patrol,
- reducing the benefit multiplier from 2.5 to 2 percent for state safety employees, and
- increasing the period for calculating final average salary from 1 year to 3 years.

Member contributions: In fiscal year 2010-2011, most CalPERS member contributions increased by between 2 and 5 percent of compensation, depending on the type of employee.

Funding changes: The CalPERS board temporarily adjusted the actuarial smoothing methods for the system's plans from 2009 to 2011 to reduce the effects of investment losses.

Selected locally-sponsored plan

Plan basics	Sonoma County Employees' Retirement Association
As of December 31, 2010	
Active members	3,780
Beneficiaries	3,780
Members covered by Social Security?	Yes
Net assets (thousands)	$1,752,819
Contributions: Employees	$37,322
(thousands) Employers	$337,761*

Source: GAO analysis of most recent financial report.

*This includes $289 3 million in pension obligation bond proceeds.

Funding changes: The county issued $289 million of pension obligation bonds (POB) in September 2010 at an interest rate of 5.51 percent to pay down the plan's unfunded liability.

Profiles of Selected State and Local Government Pensions

Colorado and the City of Denver

Colorado
Denver

Overview of Colorado state and local retirement systems (2009)

Number of plans: 67

- State plans: 2
- Local plans: 65

Active members: 223,636

- State plans: 201,524
- Local plans: 22,112

Beneficiaries: 103,134

- State plans: 87,174
- Local plans: 15,960

Percentage of members covered by Social Security: 30

Assets (thousands): $37,072,374

- State plans: $31,969,762
- Local plans: $5,102,612

Contributions (thousands)

- Employees: $658,087
- State government: $313,999
- Local government: $1,121,023

Source: GAO analysis of most recent Census and Social Security data.

Note: Census categorizes plans as state or local based on their level of administration, not sponsorship.

Selected state-sponsored plans

Plan basics	Colorado Public Employees' Retirement Association
As of December 31, 2010	
Active members	201,095
Beneficiaries	94,017
Members covered by Social Security?	No
Net assets (thousands)	$38,405,701
Contributions: Employees	$668,131
(thousands) Employers	$908,330

Source: GAO analysis of most recent plan CAFRs.

Benefit reductions: In 2010, the state reduced postretirement cost-of-living adjustments (COLA) for future, current, and retired members. The COLA was set to zero for 2010, and future COLAs were set at 2 percent, unless the plan has a negative investment return year, in which case the COLA will be the lesser of 2 percent or the Consumer Price Index for Urban Wage Earners and Clerical Workers (CPI-W) for the next 3 years. Prior to the change, most plan members had been guaranteed an annual postretirement COLA of 3.5 percent.

Member contributions: For fiscal years 2011 and 2012, the state temporarily increased member contributions by 2.5 percent of compensation and reduced employer contributions by the same amount.

Selected locally-sponsored plan

Plan basics	Denver Employees Retirement Plan
As of December 31, 2010	
Active members	8,403
Beneficiaries	7,606
Members covered by Social Security?	Yes
Net assets (thousands)	$1,802,143
Contributions: Employees	$23,090
(thousands) Employers	$45,153

Source: GAO analysis of most recent financial report.

Benefit reductions: In 2011, the city adopted several benefit reductions for new employees hired on or after July 1, 2011, including

- increasing the minimum retirement age from 55 to 60,
- increasing the age and service requirements needed to qualify for an unreduced early retirement, and
- increasing the period used for calculating final average salary from 3 to 5 years.

Profiles of Selected State and Local Government Pensions

Georgia and Cobb County

Georgia
Cobb County

Overview of Georgia state and local retirement systems (FY 2009)

Number of plans: 34

- State plans: 9
- Local plans: 25

Active members: 392,668

- State plans: 365,274
- Local plans: 27,394

Beneficiaries: 155,462

- State plans: 140,046
- Local plans: 15,416

Percentage of members covered by Social Security: 74

Assets (thousands): $60,462,340

- State plans: $54,830,465
- Local plans: $5,631,875

Contributions (thousands)

- Employees: $680,508
- State government: $1,061,525
- Local government: $579,042

Source: GAO analysis of most recent Census and Social Security data.

Note: Census categorizes plans as state or local based on their level of administration, not sponsorship.

Selected state-sponsored plans

Plan basics	Employees' Retirement System of Georgia
As of June 30, 2011	
Active members	134,487
Beneficiaries	55,929
Members covered by Social Security?	Most (varies by plan)
Net assets (thousands)	15,479,714
Contributions: Employees	$121,742
(thousands) Employers	297,763

Source: GAO analysis of most recent plan CAFRs.

Hybrid approach: In 2008, the state adopted a hybrid approach for new employees hired after January 1, 2009, that combines defined benefit and defined contribution components.

- Defined benefit portion: The plan has a 10-year vesting period with a benefit formula based on 1 percent of highest average salary multiplied by years of service.
- Defined contribution portion: Members receive a 1 percent contribution match from state on the first 1 percent they contribute to the 401(k) plan. The state then matches half of each additional percent contributed by members up to a total maximum state match of 3 percent (based on an employee contribution of 5 percent). However, as of December 31, 2011, about 10 percent of new members have opted not to participate in this part of the plan.

Selected locally-sponsored plan

Plan basics	Cobb County Employees' Retirement System Pension Plan
As of September 30, 2010	
Active members	4,242*
Beneficiaries	1,490*
Members covered by Social Security?	Yes
Net assets (thousands)	356,696
Contributions: Employees	$10,896
(thousands) Employers	$27,068

Source: GAO analysis of most recent financial report.

*As of January 1, 2010

Hybrid approach: In 2009, the county adopted a hybrid approach for new employees hired on or after January 1, 2010, and for nonvested employees who elect to join the plan. Similar to the state's new hybrid plan, the defined benefit portion of the plan has a 10-year vesting period with a benefit formula based on 1 percent of highest average salary multiplied by years of service. The defined contribution component of the plan is voluntary, but the county matches half of the member's contribution up to 2 percent.

Illinois
Chicago

Overview of Illinois state and local retirement systems (FY 2009)

Number of plans: 457

- State plans: 6
- Local plans: 451

Active members: 633,233

- State plans: 491,283
- Local plans: 141,950

Beneficiaries: 404,194

- State plans: 292,907
- Local plans: 111,287

Percentage of members covered by Social Security: 55

Assets (thousands): $100,765,313

- State plans: $67,472,265
- Local plans: $33,293,048

Contributions (thousands)

- Employees: $2,497,390
- State government: $2,765,993
- Local government: $3,150,048

Source: GAO analysis of most recent Census and Social Security data.

Note: Census categorizes plans as state or local based on their level of administration, not sponsorship.

Profiles of Selected State and Local Government Pensions

Illinois and the City of Chicago

Selected state-sponsored plans

Plan basics	State Employees' Retirement System of Illinois As of June 30, 2010	Teachers' Retirement System of the State of Illinois As of June 30, 2011
Active members	64,143	166,013
Beneficiaries	58,392	101,288
Members covered by Social Security?	Yes	No
Net assets (thousands)	$9,201,831	$37,471,267
Contributions: Employees	$246,173	$909,577
(thousands) Employers	$1,095,546*	$2,326,029*

Source: GAO analysis of most recent plan CAFRs.

*Includes state appropriations

Benefit reductions: In 2010, the state adopted several benefit changes for new members of state plans effective January 1, 2011, including

- raising the normal retirement age from 62 to 67,
- reducing COLAs to the lesser of 3 percent or half of the annual change in the CPI and made them noncompounding, and
- capping salaries used for benefit calculations and for determining contributions at $106,800 (indexed to the lesser of 3 percent or half of the annual change in the CPI).

Funding changes: The state issued $3.5 billion of POBs in 2010 and $3.7 billion in 2011 to fund the state's annual contributions to various pension systems. Previously, in 2009, the state required its pension systems to switch from a market value (no smoothing) to a 5-year smoothing method for calculating actuarial assets and contributions.

Selected locally-sponsored plan

Plan basics As of December 31, 2010	Policemen's Annuity and Benefit Fund of Chicago
Active members	12,737
Beneficiaries	12,380
Members covered by Social Security?	No
Net assets (thousands)	$3,439,669
Contributions: Employees	$108,402
(thousands) Employers	$183,835

Source: GAO analysis of most recent financial report.

Benefit reductions: In 2010, the state also adopted similar benefit changes for local government employees, including the members of this local policemen's pension plan—except the normal retirement age for policemen was raised from 50 to 55.

Funding changes: The state enacted legislation in 2010 requiring the plan to move to an actuarially based funding method in 2015.

Profiles of Selected State and Local Government Pensions

Missouri and the City of Springfield

Missouri
Springfield

Overview of Missouri state and local retirement systems (2009)

Number of plans: 66

- State plans: 10
- Local plans: 56

Active members: 265,049

- State plans: 229,472
- Local plans: 35,577

Beneficiaries: 148,249

- State plans: 123,832
- Local plans: 24,417

Percentage of members covered by Social Security: 73

Assets (thousands): $42,604,597

- State plans: $36,489,230
- Local plans: $6,115,367

Contributions (thousands)

- Employees: $780,248
- State government: $486,439
- Local government: $1,045,550

Source: GAO analysis of most recent Census and Social Security data.

Note: Census categorizes plans as state or local based on their level of administration, not sponsorship.

Selected state-sponsored plans

Plan basics	Missouri State Employees' Retirement System	Missouri Department of Transportation and Highway Patrol Employees' Retirement System
As of June 30, 2011		
Active members	51,660	8,160
Beneficiaries	35,315	7,792
Members covered by Social Security?	Yes	Yes
Net assets (thousands)	$7,866,917	$1,555,681
Contributions: Employees	$660	$45
(thousands) Employers	$ 291,121	$150,022

Source: GAO analysis of most recent plan CAFRs.

Benefit reductions: In 2010, the state adopted several benefit changes for new employees of both these plans, effective January 1, 2011, including

- raising the normal retirement age from 62 to 67 for most employees and
- increasing the vesting period from 5 to 10 years.

Member contributions: The state also adopted changes requiring new employees to contribute 4 percent of compensation (current members do not contribute).

Funding changes: The board of the State Employees' Retirement System temporarily adjusted its actuarial smoothing methods from fiscal year 2009 to 2011 to reduce the effects of market volatility.

Selected locally sponsored plan

Plan basics	City of Springfield, Missouri Police Officers' and Fire Fighters' Retirement Fund
As of June 30, 2011	
Active members	394
Beneficiaries	497
Members covered by Social Security?	No
Net assets (thousands)	$191,168
Contributions: Employees	$2,991
(thousands) Employers	$7,859

Source: GAO analysis of most recent financial report.

Funding changes: In 2009, the city approved a 0.75-cent sales tax, all of which will go toward funding the city's Police Officers' and Fire Fighters' Retirement Fund System. The city subsequently closed this plan to new members on January 31, 2010, so police and firefighters hired after this date participate in the statewide Local Government Employees Retirement System, which is less expensive for the city.

Pennsylvania
Philadelphia

Profiles of Selected State and Local Government Pensions

Pennsylvania and the City of Philadelphia

Overview of Pennsylvania state and local retirement systems (FY 2009)

Number of plans: 1,425

- State plans: 3
- Local plans: 1422

Active members: 519,496

- State plans: 392,889
- Local plans: 126,607

Beneficiaries: 385,355

- State plans: 285,831
- Local plans: 99,524

Percentage of members covered by Social Security: 93

Assets (thousands): $86,418,676

- State plans: $68,671,589
- Local plans: $17,747,087

Contributions (thousands)

- Employees: $1,560,757
- State government: $731,634
- Local government: $1,292,358

Source: GAO analysis of most recent Census and Social Security data.

Note: Census categorizes plans as state or local based on their level of administration, not sponsorship.

Selected state-sponsored plans

Plan basics	Pennsylvania State Employees' Retirement System (SERS)	Pennsylvania Public School Employees' Retirement System (PSERS)
As of Dec 31, 2010		
Active members	109,255	279,152
Beneficiaries	111,713	194,622
Members covered by Social Security?	Most (varies by plan)	Yes
Net assets (thousands)	$25,886,102	$51,311,252
Contributions: Employees	$349,049	$1,042,707
(thousands) Employers	$273,083	$747,753

Source: GAO analysis of most recent plan CAFRs.

Benefit reductions: In 2010, the state adopted several changes for new employees of both these plans, effective January 1, 2011 for SERS and July 1, 2011 for PSERS, including

- lowering the benefit multiplier from 2.5 percent to 2 percent (with an option to maintain the 2.5 percent multiplier if the member contributes at a higher rate),
- increasing the vesting period from 5 to 10 years, and
- increasing the normal retirement age for general employees from 60 to 65.

Funding changes: In 2010, the state also capped increases in employer contribution rates to both systems at 3 percent for fiscal year 2011/2012, 3.5 percent for fiscal year 2012/2013, and 4.5 percent thereafter. The state also adjusted the actuarial methods for both systems, re-amortizing State Employees' Retirement System liabilities over 30 years and re-amortizing Public School Employees' Retirement System liabilities over 24 years using a different actuarial method.

Selected locally-sponsored plan

Plan basics	City of Philadelphia Municipal Pension Plan
As of June 30, 2010	
Active members	28,632*
Beneficiaries	35,694*
Members covered by Social Security?	Yes (except police and fire)
Net assets (thousands)	$3,501,602
Contributions: Employees	$51,570
(thousands) Employers	$312,556

Source: GAO analysis of most recent financial report.

*As of July 1, 2009

Funding changes: The city partially deferred its pension payments in fiscal year 2010 and 2011 by $150 and $90 million respectively, but must pay these amounts in addition to its future annual required amounts by 2014. The city also re-amortized its liabilities over 30 years.

Profiles of Selected State and Local Government Pensions

Utah and the City of Bountiful

Utah
Bountiful

Overview of Utah state and local retirement systems (FY 2009)

Number of plans: 7

- State plans: 6
- Local plans: 1

Active members: 108,016

- State plans: 106,261
- Local plans: 1,755

Beneficiaries: 42,390

- State plans: 42,138
- Local plans: 252

Percentage of members covered by Social Security: 92

Assets (thousands): $17,641,058

- State plans: $17,568,156
- Local plans: $72,902

Contributions (thousands)

- Employees: $36,471
- State government: $641,690
- Local government: $7,680

Source: GAO analysis of most recent Census and Social Security data.

Note: Census categorizes plans as state or local based on their level of administration, not sponsorship.

Selected state-sponsored plans

Plan basics	Utah Retirement Systems
As of December 31, 2010	
Active members	104,467
Beneficiaries	46,399
Members covered by Social Security?	Most (varies by plan)
Net assets (thousands)	$19,756,106
Contributions: Employees	$59,652
(thousands) Employers	$682,600

Source: GAO analysis of most recent plan CAFRs.

Hybrid approach: In 2010, the state adopted a new retirement plan for all government employees (except judges) hired on or after July 1, 2011, providing the option of joining a defined contribution plan or a hybrid approach. The employer contribution rate is set at 10 percent of compensation for both options (12 percent for public safety employees). For the defined contribution option, the employer contributes the full 10 percent to a 401(k), in addition to any voluntary employee contributions. For the hybrid approach, members receive a defined benefit based on 1.5 percent of highest average salary multiplied by years of service. If the actuarial calculated contribution rate for the defined benefit component is less than 10 percent, the employer deposits the difference into a 401(k) plan. If the actuarial rate exceeds 10 percent, members are required to make any additional contributions to the defined benefit component.

Funding changes: In 2009, the system's board expanded the amortization period for unfunded liabilities from an open 20 year period to a closed 25 year period and adjusted the actuarial smoothing methods to reduce the effects of market volatility.

Selected locally-sponsored plan

Plan basics	Public Safety Retirement System (Bountiful City)
As of December 31, 2010	
Active members	36
Beneficiaries	not available
Members covered by Social Security?	Yes
Net assets (thousands)	$14,998
Contributions: Employees	$-
(thousands) Employers	$485

Source: GAO analysis of most recent financial report.

Hybrid approach: The city contributes to several pension plans that are administered by the Utah Retirement Systems, including the Public Safety Retirement System. The changes adopted by the state's system, described above, apply to local government employees and employers as well. Thus, new city employees hired on or after July 1, 2011, have the same option of joining a defined contribution or a hybrid approach plan, and the city's required contributions to these plans are comparable.

Virginia
Norfolk

Overview of Virginia state and local retirement systems (FY 2009)

Number of plans: 18

- State plans: 1
- Local plans: 17

Active members: 408,196

- State plans: 346,929
- Local plans: 61,267

Beneficiaries: 176,737

- State plans: 141,746
- Local plans: 34,991

Percentage of members covered by Social Security: 94

Assets (thousands): $50,599,215

- State plans: $41,975,141
- Local plans: $8,624,074

Contributions (thousands)

- Employees: $139,892
- State government: $574,911
- Local government: $1,813,973

Source: GAO analysis of most recent Census and Social Security data.

Note: Census categorizes plans as state or local based on their level of administration, not sponsorship.

Profiles of Selected State and Local Government Pensions

Virginia and the City of Norfolk

Selected state-sponsored plans

Plan basics	Virginia Retirement System
As of June 30, 2011	
Active members	339,740
Beneficiaries	156,165
Members covered by Social Security?	Yes
Net assets (thousands)	$53,151,088
Contributions: Employees	$27,623
(thousands) Employers	$1,520,403*

Source: GAO analysis of most recent plan CAFRs.

* Includes member contributions paid by employers

Benefit reductions: In 2010, the state adopted several changes for new employees hired on or after July 1, 2010, including

- increasing the period for calculating final average salary from 3 to 5 years,
- raising the normal retirement age for general employees from age 65 to the normal Social Security retirement age (age 67 for people born since 1960),
- increasing the age and service requirements needed to qualify for an unreduced retirement benefit, and
- raising early retirement eligibility from age 50 to age 60.

Member contributions: The state also adopted changes requiring new state employees hired on or after July 1, 2010 to contribute 5 percent of compensation (current members' contributions are paid by employers). In 2011, the state passed additional changes that as of July 1, 2011 require all state employees to pay the 5 percent member contribution, not just new plan members.

Selected locally-sponsored plan

Plan basics	Employees' Retirement System of the City of Norfolk
As of June 30	2010
Active members	3,950
Beneficiaries	3,271
Members covered by Social Security?	Yes (except public safety)
Net assets (thousands)	$779,404
Contributions: Employees	$-
(thousands) Employers	$35,515

Source: GAO analysis of most recent financial report.

Member contributions: In 2010, the city adopted changes requiring new city employees hired on or after October 5, 2010, to contribute 5 percent of compensation (current members do not contribute).

Assessments of a plan's funded status are complicated by the fact that there are different ways to measure plan assets and plan liabilities for different purposes, and the methods used can vary from plan to plan.[1] Plan assets could be valued at either market value or at a "smoothed" value; smoothed values are often used with the goal of producing a pattern of employer contributions to the plan that does not fluctuate as much as the financial markets. Plan liabilities can be measured under a variety of different "actuarial cost methods." An actuarial cost method is a means of assigning the costs of projected future benefits to time periods in advance of those payments. It determines what portion of the cost of an active worker's future benefits is included in the plan's liability (also sometimes called the actuarial accrued liability or the accrued liability) at any point in time.[2] Plan liabilities also vary with the actuarial assumptions used.[3] One assumption in particular, the discount rate, has been a matter of considerable controversy.

The Discount Rate Controversy

Over the past decade, there has been a growing controversy over how the value of a plan's liabilities should be determined, and in particular, over what discount rate should be used. The discount rate determines

---

[1]Funded status is a comparison of plan assets to plan liabilities. One measure of funded status is the "funded ratio," which is calculated by dividing plan assets by plan liabilities. Another measure of funded status is the difference between plan assets and plan liabilities, that is, the dollar amount of surplus or deficit. For example, if assets are greater than liabilities, the funded ratio is greater than 100 percent and the plan has a surplus (overfunding) equal to the excess of assets over liabilities; if liabilities are greater than assets, the funded ratio is less than 100 percent and the plan has a deficit (underfunding, or unfunded liability) equal to the excess of liabilities over assets.

[2]As examples, three such cost methods, as they would apply to common final-average-salary benefit formulas, are 1. "unit credit"—The accrued liability is based on the worker's service to date and current average salary—2. "projected unit credit"—The accrued liability is based on the worker's service to date and projected average salary at retirement—3. "entry age normal"—The worker's service and salary are both projected to retirement to estimate a projected benefit. The cost of this benefit is allocated over the worker's entire service (both past and projected future) as a level percentage of his or her salary. The accrued liability is the value of these allocated costs accumulated up to the point of the worker's service to date.

[3]Actuarial assumptions are needed to project the amount, likelihood, and timing of future benefits and to determine their present value, and include both economic and demographic assumptions. Economic assumptions typically include those for inflation, future salary increases, and the discount rate. Demographic assumptions typically include those for the likelihood of termination of employment, age of retirement, form of benefit elected, and longevity.

some measure of "current value" (or "present value") for pension benefits that are not payable until various points in the future. The higher the assumed discount rate, the lower the present value; conversely, the lower the assumed discount rate, the higher the present value. Thus, for example, a pension liability based on a 4 percent discount rate will be higher than the same liability based on an 8 percent discount rate. Because pension obligations extend far into the future, the discount rate is applied over a long period of time. As a result, the effect of the discount rate on pension liability measures can be substantial.

The discount rate controversy is an argument over two basic approaches to setting a plan's discount rate: (1) basing the discount rate on the expected long-term return on plan assets (which, in recent years, often would produce discount rates between 7 and 8 percent), or (2) basing the discount rate on relevant interest rates in the bond market (which, in recent years, often would produce discount rates around 4 percent). The controversy is over which of these two approaches is the appropriate one for measuring the present value of the obligations of public sector pension plans.[4]

(1) Basing the discount rate on the expected long-term return on plan assets. In this approach, the higher expected market returns on risky assets such as stocks is incorporated into the discount rate. As such, the discount rate varies with the characteristics of the plan's asset allocation, so that adopting a riskier investment policy can increase the discount rate and thereby lower liabilities and contributions.

- Those advocating for this approach argue that this rate provides the best estimate of the likely cost to finance the plan's pension obligation. They say that assuming a discount rate lower than a plan's expected rate of return would lead to higher contributions and thus overcharge the current generation.

- Those critical of this approach contend that using the expected rate of return takes credit for anticipated returns on risky investments before

---

[4]For some, the appropriate choice of discount rate will depend on the purpose for which the resulting liability measure will be used. For example, some would argue that an expected return on plan assets is the appropriate discount rate for funding purposes, while a bond-like interest rate is the appropriate discount rate for accounting purposes. Others might argue for one or the other for both purposes.

such returns actually occur, and passes on the associated risk to future generations. As such, using expected rates of return could understate the cost of pension benefits and potentially lead to excessive benefit promises. In addition, it may create an incentive to adopt riskier investment policies.

(2) Basing the discount rate on relevant interest rates in the bond market. In this approach, pension promises are viewed as "bond-like," and so are valued similarly to how the financial markets value fixed income instruments of similar duration and credit quality.

- Those advocating for this approach contend that the value of a plan's liability should be based on the characteristics of that liability, and not on the characteristics of any assets put aside to finance the liability. They say that while financial markets are volatile and not necessarily always rational, there is no better, objective way to measure the value of a pension promise than how the market currently values an obligation with similar characteristics

- Those critical of this approach hold that a "market" measure of plan promises is not relevant and thus should not be used in an ongoing pension plan. They contend that this approach would severely overstate pension costs and could lead to distorted funding, investment, and benefits policies.

Changes Currently Being Proposed

Both the Governmental Accounting Standards Board (GASB) and the Actuarial Standards Board (ASB) have issued exposure drafts proposing comprehensive revisions to their standards regarding measuring and reporting pension obligations. [5] Under current GASB accounting standards, the discount rate must be the expected return on plan assets. The GASB proposals, if enacted, would set the overall discount rate equal to a composite of (1) the expected return on plan assets to the extent that the plan is funded or projected to be funded, and (2) a high-quality municipal bond rate to the extent that some plan benefits are not expected to be funded in advance. In practice, this blended discount rate is expected to be close to the current basis—that is, the expected return on plan assets—for most plans. The GASB proposals would also require

---

[5]GASB exposure draft of revisions to Statement 27 issued June 2011; ASB exposure drafts of revisions to ASOP 4 and to ASOP 27 issued January 2012.

the use of a single, uniform actuarial cost method; [6] and they would use the current market value of plan assets, rather than a smoothed value, in determining a plan's deficit or surplus, which would be reported on the government entity's balance sheet.

Among other things, the ASB proposals, if enacted, would add additional disclosure requirements regarding funded status, including a requirement that whenever a funded status is disclosed using a smoothed value of assets, the corresponding statistic based on the market value of assets would also have to be disclosed; they would also require new disclosures regarding the type of liability measure used and the rationale for and reasonableness of the underlying actuarial assumptions. In addition, they would clarify that either approach to the discount rate is acceptable, with appropriate disclosure.

---

[6]The uniform actuarial cost method would be the "entry age normal" method, which is the method already used by most public sector plans. See prior footnote for a further description of actuarial cost methods.

Appendix III: GAO Contacts and Staff Acknowledgments

GAO Contact	Barbara D. Bovbjerg, (202) 512-7215 or bovbjergb@gao.gov, or Stanley J. Czerwinski, (202) 512-6806 or czerwinskis@gao.gov.
Staff Acknowledgments	In addition to the contacts named above, Margie K. Shields, Assistant Director; Thomas James, Assistant Director; William Colvin, Analyst-in-Charge; Robert Yetvin; and Andrea Yohe made significant contributions to this report. Susan Bernstein; James Bennett; Kathy Leslie; Frank Todisco; Walter Vance; Roger Thomas; and Sheila McCoy also made important contributions.

GAO's Mission	The Government Accountability Office, the audit, evaluation, and investigative arm of Congress, exists to support Congress in meeting its constitutional responsibilities and to help improve the performance and accountability of the federal government for the American people. GAO examines the use of public funds; evaluates federal programs and policies; and provides analyses, recommendations, and other assistance to help Congress make informed oversight, policy, and funding decisions. GAO's commitment to good government is reflected in its core values of accountability, integrity, and reliability.
Obtaining Copies of GAO Reports and Testimony	The fastest and easiest way to obtain copies of GAO documents at no cost is through GAO's website (www.gao.gov). Each weekday afternoon, GAO posts on its website newly released reports, testimony, and correspondence. To have GAO e-mail you a list of newly posted products, go to www.gao.gov and select "E-mail Updates."
Order by Phone	The price of each GAO publication reflects GAO's actual cost of production and distribution and depends on the number of pages in the publication and whether the publication is printed in color or black and white. Pricing and ordering information is posted on GAO's website, http://www.gao.gov/ordering.htm. Place orders by calling (202) 512-6000, toll free (866) 801-7077, or TDD (202) 512-2537. Orders may be paid for using American Express, Discover Card, MasterCard, Visa, check, or money order. Call for additional information.
Connect with GAO	Connect with GAO on Facebook, Flickr, Twitter, and YouTube. Subscribe to our RSS Feeds or E-mail Updates. Listen to our Podcasts. Visit GAO on the web at www.gao.gov.
To Report Fraud, Waste, and Abuse in Federal Programs	Contact: Website: www.gao.gov/fraudnet/fraudnet.htm E-mail: fraudnet@gao.gov Automated answering system: (800) 424-5454 or (202) 512-7470
Congressional Relations	Katherine Siggerud, Managing Director, siggerudk@gao.gov, (202) 512-4400, U.S. Government Accountability Office, 441 G Street NW, Room 7125, Washington, DC 20548
Public Affairs	Chuck Young, Managing Director, youngc1@gao.gov, (202) 512-4800 U.S. Government Accountability Office, 441 G Street NW, Room 7149 Washington, DC 20548

www.ingramcontent.com/pod-product-compliance
Lightning Source LLC
Chambersburg PA
CBHW080910290526
45795CB00007BA/2487